JULY

2 Liberals resign from government.

3 Germans counter-attack. Kerensky offensive turns into disastrous defeat. Demonstrations in Petrograd demanding "All Power to the Soviets."

4 Kronstadt sailors arrive in Petrograd, join demonstrations. Lenin calls for self-restraint. Government troops fire on armed demonstrators.

5 Government raids Bolshevik headquarters and *Pravda* offices. Newspaper is shut down. Many Bolshevik leaders arrested. Lenin goes into hiding.

8 Kerensky becomes prime minister. Lenin flees Petrograd.

10 Petrograd Soviet issues decree supporting reorganized Provisional Government. Trotsky arrested.

16 Government orders civilians disarmed.

17 Kerensky appoints Kornilov commander in chief.

23 Second coalition government formed.

26 Bolshevik Party congress begins.

AUGUST

9 Elections to Constituent Assembly postponed.

12 State Conference in Moscow begins.

20 Bolsheviks score major gains in Petrograd municipal elections.

25 Kornilov coup attempt begins. Government orders evacuation of Petrograd.

26 Kornilov's demands delivered to Kerensky.

27 Grain prices double. Committee for the People's Struggle Against Counter-revolution organized and armed.

30 Kornilov defeated. Kerensky becomes commander in chief.

31 Petrograd Soviet passes first resolution of Bolshevik majority.

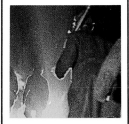

SEPTEMBER

1 Russia proclaimed a republic.

4 Trotsky freed from jail.

5 Moscow Soviet passes a Bolshevik motion.

8 Trotsky elected chairman of Petrograd Soviet.

14 Democratic conference opens. Transformation of Petrograd's workers' militia into Red Guards.

19 Moscow Soviet elects Bolshevik-dominated executive committee.

23 Nationwide rail strikes begin.

25 Kerensky reshuffles cabinet.

OCTOBER

16 Military Revolutionary Committee formed.

21 Petrograd garrison acknowledges Soviet as sole power and Military Revolutionary Committee as immediate organ of authority.

24 October insurrection begins. Government closes left-wing newspapers. Red Guards mobilize. Lenin emerges from hiding.

24–25 Military Revolutionary Committee seizes key communications points.

25 Second Congress of Soviets opens; Bolsheviks have majority. Kerensky flees Winter Palace. Cruiser *Aurora* fires round of blanks. Winter Palace shelled from Peter and Paul Fortress. Overthrow of Provisional Government proclaimed.

26 Revolutionaries take Winter Palace and arrest ministers. Rightists and liberals form anti-Bolshevik Committee for Salvation of Country and Revolution. Declaration of Peace.

30 Petrograd Red Guards defeat counter-revolutionary Cossacks under Kerensky.

NOVEMBER

1 Kerensky flees Gatchina, narrowly avoiding capture.

2 Declaration on rights of nationalities. Moscow revolutionaries take the Kremlin.

7 Nationalization of state bank.

9 Suppression of liberal and right-wing newspapers. Liberal leaders arrested. *Pravda* publishes secret treaties.

10 Ranks abolished in armed forces and civil society.

11 Extraordinary Congress of Peasants' Deputies opens.

12 Voting for Constituent Assembly begins.

14 Decree on workers' control.

17 Nationalization of private property begins.

22 Preliminary armistice with Germany and Austria-Hungary.

26 Government bureaucrats strike and are denounced as "enemies of the people."

DECEMBER

2 Supreme Council of National Economy formed.

7 Brest-Litovsk peace conference opens. CHEKA (All-Russian Extraordinary Commission for the Struggle Against Sabotage and Counter-revolution) organized and headed by Felix Dzerzhinsky.

12 Left Socialist Revolutionaries join government.

14 Private banks nationalized.

17 Marriage and divorce laws reformed. Civil ceremony decreed only legal form.

22 Abolition of zemstvo, local self-government units.

30 Preparations for New Year in world's first socialist country.

RUSSIA
1917
THE
UNPUBLISHED REVOLUTION

RUSSIA 1917

THE UNPUBLISHED REVOLUTION

by Jonathan Sanders
Foreword by Vitaly Korotich

ABBEVILLE PRESS   PUBLISHERS   NEW YORK

EDITOR'S NOTE

Unless otherwise indicated, Julian calendar (old style) dates
are given throughout. The Julian calendar was followed in
Russia until February 1918, when the Gregorian calendar was
adopted. Because the twentieth-century Julian calendar is thirteen days behind the Gregorian calendar, the October Revolution, which began on 24 October (old style), is now
celebrated on 7 November (new style).

To facilitate the pronunciation of Russian names, a modified
version of the New York Public Library's transliteration system
has been used.

The assistance of Robert H. Davis, George Estafy, and
Serge Glebov at the Slavic and Baltic Division of the New
York Public Library is gratefully acknowledged.

Front cover and frontispiece:
The faces of revolution: a May Day demonstration in Petro-
grad, 18 April 1917.
Page 12:
The Revolution begins as Petrograd's women workers demon-
strate on International Women's Day, 23 February 1917. The
banner reads: "Increased Rations for Soldiers' Families."
Back cover:
Twelve scenes of the revolutionary year 1917.

EDITOR: JACQUELINE DECTER
DESIGNER: JOEL AVIROM
PRODUCTION EDITOR: AMY HANDY
PRODUCTION MANAGER: DANA COLE
MAP BY SOPHIE KITTREDGE
CYRILLIC LETTERING BY PAUL SHAW

First edition
Library of Congress Cataloging-in-Publication Data

Sanders, Jonathan.
    Russia, 1917 : the unpublished revolution / by Jonathan
Sanders.   p.   cm.
    Bibliography: p.
    Includes index.
    ISBN 0-89659-775-X
    1. Soviet Union—History—Revolution,
1917–1921.   2. Soviet Union—History—Revolution,
1917–1921—Pictorial works. I. Title.
DK265.S2928   1989
947.084'1—dc19   89-267
                                           CIP

Printed and bound in Italy.

This book is dedicated to
Solomon Wank and the late Samuel E. Allen,
inspirational teachers and friends.

ACKNOWLEDGMENTS

Alexander Meledin's love of photography, tenacious research skills, and knowledge made this book possible. Like the wonderful people in charge of many Soviet archives, he values photographs as windows into the past, believing that they make the animating spirit of bygone times come alive again. Without the care of the archivists, their darkroom technicians, and their thoughtful colleagues at VAAP (the Soviet Copyright Agency), including Alexander Rounkov, Gennady Zareev, and Sergei Abramov, this book would not have been conceivable and could never have seen the light of day. My wonderful editor at Abbeville Press, Jackie Decter, needed all of her skills—including patience, persistence, and diplomacy—in dealing with a very idiosyncratic, peripatetic, opinionated author. Brezhnev would have awarded her medals and named a city after her. My thanks are more humble, but more sincere. The people at Belka International used their exceptional contacts and negotiating and publicity skills in the realization of this project. In the Moscow office, Viktor Khrolenko, Cynthia Rosenberger, Natasha, and Demyan nurtured me. In the New York office, Belka President Marina Albee and Creative Director Kenny Schaffer were inspirational. Much of this book was written while I was at the W. Averell Harriman Institute for Advanced Study of the Soviet Union. Colette and Marshall Shulman encouraged me to pursue my interest in matching words and pictures. My supportive colleagues Robert Legvold, Richard Ericson, Eugene Beshenkovsky, Mark Von Hagen, Elizabeth Valkenier, and William Harkins made the institute a hospitable place to work. Most important, my imaginative, dependable, long-time research and teaching assistant, John Copp, diligently tracked down obscure references, found little-known photographs, sketched out the chronology, and lent me his profound insights into the anarchist movement. Penny Zaleta, my wonderful and principled assistant, helped in more ways than I can acknowledge. Word-processing whiz Paul Ellis turned computer glitches into prose. Many of the ideas in this book were born and nurtured over several years in a seminar I led on 1917. I am very grateful to the students in that seminar, who taught me a great deal. I also worked on this book while at CBS News. In Moscow, then bureau chief Wyatt Andrews and his wife, Amy, extended exceptional hospitality and curiosity, as did his successor, Barry Peterson, and Jan Chorlton Peterson. Boris Zakharov and the crack bureau staff always lent their assistance, as did my good friends in the CBS Special Events unit and the patient folks in the Northeast Bureau. By example, Susan Zirinsky showed me that it was possible to work on many projects at once. During the long period I worked on this book I got by with a little help from my friends, especially Francis Wcislo, Robert Edelman, Daniel Field, Andrew Verner, Stephen Cohen, Janet and Alexander Rabinowitch, Steve Jacobs, Ivan T.C., Rubin Ivanovich, Bruce Elleman, Larry Chesler, Brat de Puss, Dan Orlovsky, Joseph Ritchie, and Walter Clebowicz. Most importantly, wonderful Mary Rosenfeld shared my enthusiasm for this project and much else.

Moscow
30 March 1989

CONTENTS

At first it happened only in our country. You were living through different events. In a world where television was still unknown and even radios were scarce, people got their news slowly. With few exceptions, the photographs reproduced in this book did not create a stir in their own time. It's we today who need them. But back then . . .

In 1917 the English established the Order of the British Empire, a railroad bridge almost two thousand feet long was built in Quebec, and a one-hundred-inch telescope went up in California. While Richard Strauss was organizing music festivals in Salzburg, the world's first bomber plane was being produced in Germany. While the eastern and western halves of Australia were being linked by a railroad line, the future Nobel laureate T.S. Eliot was finishing his "Prufrock."

That's when our Revolution took place. There were even two of them: the one Western historians call the Bourgeois-Liberal Revolution in February (March, new style), which caused Tsar Nicholas II to abdicate his throne, and the Bolshevik Revolution in October (November, new style), which laid the foundation of a completely new life and time. Russia was convulsed by revolutions the likes of which—in scale and in the profound changes they brought—humanity had perhaps never known. Russia subjected itself to a socialist experiment that would yield ambiguous results and be analyzed for a long time to come. In the course of a single year, 1917, the country went from a monarchy to a republic to a dictatorship. It even managed to survive for a while under dual power, with a bourgeois Provisional Government and the Soviet of Workers' and Soldiers' Deputies existing side by side.

Russian history is arhythmic. A lot goes on, sometimes at a lethargic pace, which gives rise to the sleeping bear metaphor, sometimes at great speed. Our history doesn't carry all its children to full term, but once born, they tend to move energetically, even run, from the very moment of delivery. The Revolution ripened gradually and deliberately, then exploded like an earthquake, traversing in just a few months a path that was inconceivable by history's traditional standards. Look at these photographs—you won't see a single indifferent face in them. Everyone is either ecstatic or deeply preoccupied. Everyone is actively engaged. Many were already linked by blood to the events—for them it was kill or be killed, sometimes both.

The majority of these people are no longer living. Time is pitiless; revolutions devour their own children and creators; our Revolution was particularly fierce in this regard. It mercilessly liquidated those whose efforts had brought it to fruition. Still, for a while, for several months, a spirit of unity prevailed, the murderers didn't as yet recognize the faces of their future victims. Huge throngs chanted universal love, rejection of the old order, and sympathy for their suffering brothers. In the maelstrom of rebellion the most exalted dreams got mixed up with the most down-to-earth ambitions. In this respect lessons can be drawn from the Russian Revolution only after the most dispassionate examination. Dreamers and cynics, pragmatists and visionaries, idealists and thieves—the blendings were varied, at times monstrous: the exceptionally erudite Lenin; Bukharin with his aptitude for refined theoretical reasoning; the horrendously ignorant but no less power-hungry Stalin; and Trotsky with his irrepressible desire to have everything at once and to spare no one in the process. Characters and passions Shakespearian in breadth; farce that exploded into tragedy; and tens of millions of people who were genuinely drawn to a better life.

There were so many people, and so many blueprints. There was so much shooting, so much singing, so much arguing.

You're probably tired of reading encyclopedias, novels, and memoirs, where the Russian Revolution is recounted in names and dates. This book is by no means a story about the Revolution's leaders and famous participants. Rather, it is a mirror, frozen in time—a whole country is looking at you from the photographs. This was the first revolution in human history to be documented in such detail.

You and I were welded together by this revolution. No other series of events in the twentieth century brought Russia into such close contact with Europe. Other governments and peoples made no secret of their response to the Revolution. Countries that were opposed sent troops to intervene in northern and far eastern Russia. Workers in Italy and France held mass meetings to express their solidarity with Russian workers, while homegrown revolts ripened in Germany and Hungary. All the bloodbaths of the twentieth century have tried to justify themselves as a struggle for the common good. But it was the Russian Revolution that first introduced the idea of sacrifice. The Russians believed in this concept more than anyone else. And the Russian Revolution triumphed because of this faith. Philosophical utopianism became intertwined with Christian precepts, the thirst for blood with the thirst for justice, and a thrust toward the future with the desire to come to terms with current reality.

We always knew how to dream. The vision of a bright future, as a rule, exerts a much more powerful and consistent pull on people than does the more prosaic challenge of working hard for the here and now. The Russians as a nation carried and nurtured the dream of a great realm of justice, even Justice writ large, throughout their long-suffering, painfully difficult and bloody history. This entitled them, in 1917, to sever all the Gordian knots of their fate in one fell swoop. A country that had existed for centuries on the periphery of world history, unable to keep pace with, or reluctant to enter, the mainstream, a country both "wretched and bountiful," "powerful and impotent," in the words of one of Russia's greatest nineteenth-century poets, suddenly exploded into the river of time, made it seethe, dammed it up, and significantly changed the direction of its current. You are now holding in your hands the photo album of 1917's witnesses and participants. Cast a glance at the turbulent sea of Russia's national history as it was converging more and more closely with the destiny of other peoples.

Theoreticians explain why the Revolution succeeded in Russia and couldn't have been as successful anywhere else. Perhaps they are right, because the disparity in material wealth in the country was enormous, there were many landless peasants, and the desire to take from the haves and give to the have-nots took hold on most levels of society. The Russian nobility, moreover, was quite unique. They displayed a marked propensity for sacrifice and self-abasement, often without regarding this as any kind of heroism.

Nowhere else in Europe, I think, was there at that time such a striking gulf between the highly educated, talented "upper crust"—which, despite its many profound failings, had managed to cultivate and preserve the most brilliant minds of the age—and the most unenlightened peasant masses, more than half of whom were illiterate; between the most luxurious Petersburg soirées and the impoverished conditions of laborers in the country's hinterland. In our country the twentieth century lived cheek by jowl with the eighteenth, even with the Middle Ages. Between two such poles wasn't it inevitable that the spark of revolutionary fire would ignite? It's hard to say, because at the same time there were several unrealized social upheavals lurking in the depths of Russian society. Down through the ages this enormous land had had no inkling of parliamentary government; there had never been a bourgeois revolution in Russia; the effects of the Renaissance had been, at the very least, somewhat idiosyncratic. And the country crept into the twentieth century in this transitional state between the Middle Ages and more modern times. That's why the Revolution occurred simultaneously in many different social and historical strata, and often meant different things to different groups.

The people who look at you from the pages of this book were thinking not only of themselves. The Russian passion to do good for humankind, the age-old slogan of Slavic revolutions—"For your freedom and ours!" —gave particular force to the messianic mission of the crowd. The people in these photographs were thinking about you, too.

Those who were obsessed with the thirst for justice had precise prescriptions for attaining their ideal. History has proved to what extent their dream was unattainable, in what ways their plans were not well thought out, in what ways their methods were flawed or mistaken. But the majority of the people you see in this book were struggling for a goal that was pure and honest, for a world without slaves or masters, for a kind of paradise for themselves and for humanity. It seems to me that nowhere else in the world, either before or since the demonstrations, mass meetings, strikes, and battles of 1917, have there been movements of such scope, uniting people around a dream whose methods of realization even to this day each person envisions in his or her own way. Many Europeans turned out to be much more practical than these people; they implemented a number of the Russians' ideas and instituted many changes. But Europe might not have been able to accomplish so much so quickly without the jolt that Russia gave the world in 1917. In large part, I believe, the new role of labor unions, the changing relationship between employers and workers, and the democratization of social processes began there—in the public squares, streets, and meeting halls that are depicted in this book. When we speak today about a united Europe, about the unification of all humankind, let's remember that the Russian Revolution of 1917 was also waged under universal slogans. Large popular upheavals are always universal: the people who backed Cromwell in England, who brought about the great French Revolution, who created the February and October Revolutions in Russia, played a part in the destiny of many nations. The visionary brain of a giant can't always work out detailed means for achieving its ends; the transformation and realization of its ideas can take centuries.

The February Revolution was not able to solve the problems in one fell swoop, yet the people demanded immediate change: give land to the peasants, make peace at any price, settle the nationalities question, satisfy the workers' demands. The October Revolution, the socialist, Bolshevik one, triumphed by issuing all the necessary decrees, by cutting all the knots with one blow. We understood only later what a great distance there often is between an idea and its realization. But that question lies beyond the scope of this book.

Demonstrations involving half a million people raged in Petrograd and Moscow in the summer of 1917. The crowds were not yet divided by the specter of imminent civil war. In the photographs you see these people united; many of them would soon become implacable enemies and they would kill or attempt to kill one another. Later on the censors, the powers that be, would try to erase some of these people from the national memory forever; about twenty years after the events recorded in this book the photographs began to be retouched, and some of the faces were removed from them. In the land of revolution as religion, fraudulent icons of the miracle workers made their appearance.

It is important to remember that the crowds milling about in the streets and public squares of revolutionary Russia consisted not only of Russian citizens but of people from all over. The whirlwinds of world war and of world revolution collided, giving birth to unprecedented cyclones. Sometimes the party affiliation of the participants in these events could be determined only after their deaths, but then, in those days the whole planet pulsated in a web of pseudonyms, family names, real and imaginary fates. And they were buried in mass graves: the bullets didn't distinguish their victims by nationality; they penetrated the pages of any passport. The universality of the Russian uprising made brothers of its participants both in life and in death.

There's no need for any retouching. Preserve these photos in their original form. Try to understand these people. The majority of them wanted to change the world for the better—immediately, and once and for all. Today we know that instantaneous changes are by no means always stable. But to learn this we had to live through a great deal and rethink a lot of things. Political hindsight is always instructive. Let's leaf through this book once again, and, as we look into the faces of people who have long since departed from this world, we'll recognize in them ourselves and those who stand alongside us today. We're not the same as we were before; we've been enriched by our experience; we want happiness; we're so much like them.

Vitaly Korotich
Editor in chief of *Ogonyok*

Translated from the Russian by Gerald Mikkelson

ПРИБАВКУ ПАЙКА
СЕМЬЯМЪ СОЛДАТЪ
ЗАЩИТНИКАМЪ СВОБОДЫ
И НАРОДНОГО МІРА.

RUSSIA 1917
THE UNPUBLISHED REVOLUTION

Russians had long anticipated revolution. Throughout the latter part of the nineteenth century, radicals, reformers, conservatives, and court councillors alike predicted an end to the old order. Just after the turn of the century, the decidedly unrevolutionary Moscow city fathers proclaimed: "An all-Russian choir is chanting a funeral prayer for the Old Russia. . . . the tenacious historical evolution begun half a century ago is irresistibly rushing to reach its goal."[1] Though many sensed that Russia was hurtling forward, propelled by some inexorable force, no one seemed able to control it or determine its course. The time, timing, and timeliness of revolution surprised ruler and ruled alike.

The changes wrought in the revolutionary year 1917 were dramatic departures from the past. Russians turned their world upside down, not merely changing rulers, but utterly revising basic values. Even the fundamental concept of personal identity—the answer to the question "Who are you?"—underwent an abrupt transformation. For centuries Russians had identified themselves according to a complex system of hereditary, castelike ranks or estates in which one's father's status (peasant, merchant, minor noble, etc.) determined who one was. This rigid hierarchy, wholly sanctioned by law, formed the core of Russia's social system. It gave everyone a role in serving the state. As one keen observer commented in 1859, "Every estate has its own role in the state: the clergy prays, the nobles serve in war and peace, the peasants plow and feed the people, and the merchants are the means that provide each [estate] with what it needs."[2] Suddenly this ascriptive system, which had long slowed the development of society, gave way to broad democracy and self-determination. In the jargon of social scientists, one might say that the Revolution's universalism (or more precisely, its pretension to universalism) destroyed traditional particularism. Traditionalism gave way to modernism. But it was Russian tradition that conditioned its peculiar form of modernization. The heritage of the past, in one of 1917's great paradoxes, formed the very forces smashing it.

The dynamic of any revolution highlights, in the starkest contrast, the tension between continuity and change that forms the groundwork of all history. In the late nineteenth and early twentieth centuries, backward, agrarian Russia courted disaster by trying to meet the challenge of industrialization while maintaining its old social and political structures. The tsars tried to modernize obsolete systems, but they did so in a very Russian way. After decades of inaction they suddenly and sporadically imposed catch-up reforms imported from the West or based on Western models. Natural, indigenous growth of ideas or institutions rarely occurred. Moderation, compromise, and middle ground were absent. Extremism flourished: opulence and poverty; great, cultured cities and abysmally primitive villages; a desiccated nobility and a vibrant working class; avant-garde thinking and religious superstition—the oppositions were seemingly endless, lending a very Russian character to the country's emergence into the industrial world.

A comprehensive definition of *Russianness* would require a tome filled with quotations from those great scholars of the subject: Gogol, Turgenev, Tolstoy, Dostoevsky, Tyutchev, Gorky, and others. Only some sense of Russia's unique character can be provided here. Let us begin with the word *Russian*. This seemingly simple word brings us into contact with a language that is not exactly congruent with our own. Two distinct words, *russkii* and *rossiisskii*, are both translated as "Russian" in English. The first, *russkii*, refers to a national grouping, the people sometimes called the Great Russians, not necessarily because they are wonderful but to distinguish them from other Slavic groups such as the Little Russians (Ukrainians) or the White Russians (Belorussians). The second word, *rossiisskii*, refers to all the peoples, nationalities, and territories that comprised the tsar's empire. At the time of the first modern census, in 1897, the Russian (*rossiisskii*) Empire had a population of 128,000,000, made up of some 200 nationalities speaking 146 or so different tongues. In addition to Russians there were Ukrainians, Belorussians, Jews, Lithuanians, Armenians, Georgians, Bashkirs, Tadzhiks, Uzbeks, Chukchi, etc. All of these peoples lived in a huge country of 8,550,000 square miles, which is only 50,000 square miles less than the Soviet Union today and more than twice

the present size of the United States (3,618,467 square miles). Thus, the country known as Russia was an enormous multinational state whose population was largely, but not exclusively, Russian (*russkii*).

The harsh physical world these Russians inhabited helped shape their character. Without fear of exaggeration or contradiction, we can say that Russia's physical setting has constituted the most stable feature in its history. The heart of central Russia is a cold, northern land where precipitation comes mostly in the form of snow and nature provides scant resources for agricultural prosperity.

The great nineteenth-century historian V. O. Klyuchevsky (1841–1911) observed:

> There is one thing the Great Russian believes in: that one must cherish the clear summer working day, that nature allows him insufficient time for agriculture and that Russia's brief summer can be further shortened by unseasonably fierce storms. This compels the Great Russian peasant to hustle to exert himself strenuously so as to get as much done quickly and quit the field in good time and then to be at leisure to do nothing throughout the fall and winter. Thus the Great Russian has accustomed himself to excessive bursts of energy; he has learned to work fast, feverishly, and intensively, and to rest during the enforced idleness of fall and winter. No nation in Europe is capable of such intense exertion over short periods of time as the Great Russian. But probably nowhere in Europe do we also find such a lacking of the habit for even moderate, well distributed and steady work as in this very same Great Russian.[3]

This propensity for accomplishing things in feverishly intense explosions of activity rather than through slow, steady effort is known as *shturmovshchina* ("storming") and it characterizes the Russian sense of tempo and timing. It is as evident in the work habits of Soviet citizens today as in the rhythms of Russian history. Russia experienced long periods of inaction. When change came, it raced forward at a furious pace.

Peter the Great, ruled
■ 1694–1725.

The state acted as the primary agent of change. Time and again Russia demonstrated how different it was from Western Europe or America, where the interests of individuals set historical events in motion. In contrast to change in these lands, where concern for individual rights, fair taxation and representation, or the economic privileges of a rising liberal middle class bubbled up spontaneously from below and forced rulers to alter their course, in Russia innovation was ordered from the top down.

The state acted against society instead of interacting with it. Strong tsars commanded changes, but orders could only create structures not shock absorbers for the unanticipated consequences of those changes. So the state had to implement reforms through coercive action against society rather than through cooperation with it. The quintessential actor promoting the state at the expense of society was Peter the Great. Peter came to power in 1694 determined to modernize Russia. He spent a lifetime reorganizing the country and remodeling its institutions. He borrowed ideas, technology, and experts from Western Europe. This great reformer even forced his servitors to westernize their appearance by shaving their beards and adopting western dress. He promoted men on the basis of ability and rewarded officeholders with noble titles, estates, and serfs.

While Western Europe was beginning to release its peasants from feudal subjugation in the late sixteenth century, the Russian tsars, eager for sources of wealth with which to reward their commanders and servitors, tied the most humble of their population to the land that they freely distributed to nobles. Russian peasants were barely surviving while supporting their lords, who in turn supported the state. The peasants endured a serfdom hardly distinguishable from slavery. A noble counted his wealth not by the size of his estate but by the number of "souls" he owned. The serf lived at the mercy of the master's whims. No effective law protected the serf from excesses, no code of common consent or common civility among serf owners prevented mistreatment of peasants. Talk of whipping, rape, Siberian exile, and other brutalities shocked foreign visitors. Of course, the most wealthy and influential nobles lived in the capitals, St. Petersburg and Moscow, leaving the peasants to bear up against the mud, disease, and isolation of the countryside. The Russian village, as Tolstoy's "Morning of a Landlord" and Turgenev's *Sportsman's Sketches* illustrate, was a peasant world. The Russian nobleman was almost an outsider on his own ancestral estate.

Serfdom left a deep imprint both psychologically and economically on serf owners and their human property. Nobles lived parasitically off their serfs. A subsistence- and consumption-oriented economic system, serfdom depended on the peasants' traditional habits of cultivation: superstition, folk wisdom, and age-old patterns dictated how and when they farmed. Science played no role and cost accounting was unheard of. In fact, noblemen had no idea how their own estates—the basis of their livelihood—operated. At best, stewards supervised peasant production. The system fostered routine and discouraged any nascent entrepreneurial spirit. Experience bred fear in the nobles: fear of changes and of the peasants' elemental wrath. Nobles knew well that "Russian revolts, senseless and merciless," as the great poet Alexander Pushkin called them, threatened their very lives. Fed up with oppression, the peasants periodically saw in a messianic leader— often a rogue pretending to be the tsar—a chance to escape the horrors of serfdom by rising against their oppressors.

Starting on Russia's southern periphery during the sixteenth and seventeenth centuries, peasant

Peasants drinking tea from
■ a samovar, late 1800s.

The steward of a
■ nobleman's estate.

mobs created paths of death and destruction as they marched toward Moscow. Nobles were tortured, hanged, decapitated, and mutilated. Rampaging peasants raped women, razed towns, and torched manor houses. They obliterated any symbol of intrusive, alien European civilization and anything that smacked of state-imposed rule or bureaucracy. They smashed dishes, porcelain, card tables, and burned title deeds, account books, tax rolls. Such peasant uprisings, or jacqueries, attacked the foundations of Russian autocracy. The general who put down the last major peasant revolt, led by the Cossack Emelyan Pugachev in the 1770s, recognized that it was "a revolt of the poor against the rich, of the slaves against the masters."[4] Pugachev personified the peasants' general indignation. It took a skilled army, combined with the treacherous greed of Pugachev's own supporters (who betrayed him for a huge reward), to undo direct assault on the noblemen. Catherine the Great, that paragon of enlightened absolutism, ruthlessly punished those involved. Pugachev himself was tried in Moscow and beheaded. His head was mounted on a stake, his body quartered and paraded around the city for all to see; his native village was burned to the ground. Official edicts banned his name. Orders from above were useless, however: Pugachev's name has lived

on in songs, folklore, and peasant legends. His bravado was immortalized in verse by such poets as Alexander Pushkin and Marina Tsvetaeva.

The specter of Pugachev, fear of *Pugachevshchina*—a massive peasant uprising smashing through the countryside's thin veneer of civilization—haunted the nobility and the autocracy. It drew the nobles and the state authorities closer together for mutual reinforcement and cemented the institution of serfdom at a time when other nations, notably Denmark, France, and Switzerland, were about to abandon similar servile institutions. Some observers, especially those examining events after the violence ended, saw the Pugachev rebellion as an act against the Europeanization and modernization of Russia, not against serfdom per se.

Thus the ghost of Pugachev was an unwitting conservative force, one prodding tsars, nobles, and bureaucrats to maintain the old order. Tsars feared that even the rumor of reform would spark a mass uprising. Throughout his reign (1825–55), Nicholas I formed ten deliberative bodies to consider freeing the serfs; all met as very "secret" committees. Serf owners, little tsars on their own estates, received constant reinforcement. Nicholas I told the St. Petersburg nobility: "I have no police, gentlemen: I don't like them; you are my police. Each of you is my steward."[5] Some claim that if Napoleon had brooked disorder and proclaimed a general emancipation of the serfs, he would have triumphed over Moscow. Discussions and considerations of an end to serfdom came to naught by the mid-nineteenth century. The government shunted aside all the secret deliberations under Nicholas I, all the plans for reform, once Western Europe's 1848 revolutions raised anxieties and prompted the "iron tsar" to act as the continent's gendarme, using the force of arms to restore the status quo. (Apropos of such interventions the poet Tyutchev remarked, "For a long time only two real forces have existed in Europe: Revolution and Russia—no transaction, no treaties, are possible between them: the existence of one is the death of the other.")

By mid-century Russia had purchased stability at the price of progress. Only a sudden blow from the outside—combined with the tsar's death—broke the cocoon suffocating the country. The Crimean War, the first major encounter between Russia and the great European powers in forty years, erupted in October 1853. The allied victories quickly dramatized Russia's backwardness. Against France and Great Britain the state failed abjectly in its most basic mission: the protection of Russian security, borders, and national interests. With "serve Russia" as his dying words to his son, Nicholas I handed over the old order to a new tsar, Alexander II, who began reforming Russia with the help of some progressive bureaucrats, placing the country very firmly on the road to 1917.

Alexander II launched his reign by announcing his intention to emancipate the serfs. In a famous statement he declared that it was better to liberate the peasants from above than to wait until they freed themselves from below. Serfs paid for their own liberation, purchasing a portion of the land they had worked and, in effect, compensating their owners for the loss of their value in a payment system that extended into the twentieth century. In other words, the peasants were not given their freedom, they bought it along with meager portions of the poorest land. But peasants also lost free use of their former landlords' woods and pastures. As time passed and the peasant population grew, the need for more land became pressing. In the short run, the state got what it wanted—an end to serfdom and a

Emelyan Pugachev (1742–75), ■ peasant uprising leader.

reassured nobility with money that hadn't depleted the state treasury. In the long run, however, this approach created a peasantry who had freed itself.

THE ERA OF GREAT REFORMS

The 1860s was a decade of liberalization and reform. The government relaxed censorship, created organs of local self-government, and reformed the judiciary, the educational system, and the military. Many of Russia's educated citizens, especially the youth, expected much more reform to come more quickly. But when the "Tsar-Liberator" failed to follow his social and administrative reforms with political liberation, his subjects turned cynical and became antigovernment.

A nihilist generation, so brilliantly depicted in Turgenev's novel *Fathers and Sons*, burst onto the scene. Soon a small group of alienated intellectuals transformed their discontent into revolutionary opposition; young men and women embraced its extremism. Totally committed to their cause, they could serve as exemplary models for fanatics everywhere. The famous 1868 broadside, "Catechism of the Revolutionary," captured their animating spirit: "The revolutionary is a doomed man. He has no interests, no affairs, no feelings, no habits, no property, not even a name. Everything in him is wholly absorbed by a single exclusive interest, a single thought, a single passion—the revolution."[6] Successive generations built underground organizations on these same principles.

A fascination with oppositional ideas quickly translated into a preoccupation with acts that would change Russia. In the 1870s radical youths embarked on missions to revolutionize the country. They based their actions on the belief that the Russian peasants were instinctive socialists. They saw the peasant commune as an egalitarian and rough democratic institution that would serve as the basis for socialism in Russia. Because of this inherent socialism, they felt, Russia could leap directly from the oppression of serfdom to a future of radiant (and utopian) equality without passing through the horrors of "capitalist" industrialization, as epitomized by that which took place in Manchester, England.

These populist radicals interpreted another Russian peasant tradition, the spontaneous uprising, or *Puga-chevshchina*, to mean that the masses were revolutionaries. All they needed was a push, a dramatic action, a spark, to catalyze them into action. Russian populism formed the matrix of political radicalism in the 1870s.

Some Russian populists argued for a coup d'état, others for redressing the wrongs done to the people by assassinating government officials. Still others eschewed violence for agitation and propaganda. Centralized and conspiratorial circles gained adherents, and underground sects spun out elaborate justifications for terrorism. Police officers, governors, and, on 1 March 1881, the tsar himself fell victim to violence. Inspired by government agents, a wave of pogroms swept Russia as Jews were blamed for the "Tsar-Liberator's" death. A period of dark reaction ensued during which the government effectively suppressed all but the most mild "small deeds," such as bringing literacy to the countryside, providing basic medical care, and introducing rudimentary

Tsar Alexander III,
■ ruled 1881–94.

techniques of modern agriculture. A few courageous souls, including Lenin's older brother, persevered. The government hung him for an attempt on the life of the new tsar, Alexander III, in 1887. The slack season of radicalism, however, coincided with a new approach toward revitalizing the economy: state-sponsored, hothouse industrialization.

Between 1887 and 1900 more than one million men and women, most of them peasants, entered the industrial labor force. The spread of factories, the growth of a working class, the prospects for progress through capitalism, combined with the collapse of terrorism's glamorous appeal, led to enthusiasm among radicals for a new revolutionary idea: Marxism. The first leaders of Russian Marxism emerged from the populist movement. They formed circles both inside the country and abroad and recruited educated people, largely from the universities. Soon they were engaged in extensive propaganda activity among the workers. In the last decade of the nineteenth century they participated in heated theoretical debates with young populists. The young Lenin, then an obscure figure in an underground Marxist circle, published his first political tract, an attack on Russian populism. These Marxist circles gave birth to the Russian Social Democratic Labor party in 1898. At the founding congress (in 1903 the party split into Bolshevik [majority] and Menshevik [minority] factions over the issue of whether the party should be made up solely of professional revolutionaries or a more mixed group), the party declared: "The farther east one goes in Europe the weaker, coarser and more cowardly becomes the bourgeoisie and the larger the cultural and political task falls to the proletariat. On its strong shoulders the Russian working class must bear and will bear the cost of winning political liberty. This is an inevitable but only an initial step toward the realization of the proletariat's great historic mission, the creation of a social order which will allow no room for the exploitation of man by man."[7]

This determined party found a ready-made constituency among Russia's rapidly expanding working classes. Cities, especially the capitals, were the core of industrial expansion and had long been the gravitational center for the country's militant youths.

Vladimir Ilich Lenin
■ in St. Petersburg, 1895.

Conditions there differed greatly from the peasant world the new urbanites had left behind. One worker described a factory neighborhood in St. Petersburg as "an entire forest of factory chimneys, throwing out clouds of black smoke obscuring the already gray Petersburg sky. The factory buildings, houses, streets, and bustling crowds of people were covered with a thick layer of soot. From all directions massive rhythmical sounds assaulted you—the rattle of huge rollers, the penetrating clank of iron bars, the heat of steam hammers which shook the earth." And living conditions offered little respite: "My room was not far from the factory in a huge stinking house. . . . We were fifteen men renting an apartment as a collective. Some were bachelors, others had wives in the countryside who looked after the land. I was put in a small dark room without windows—in other words, a closet. It was filthy and stuffy, full of cockroaches and bugs and smelled acutely of 'humanity.' In this closet stood two wooden cots. My fellow villager . . . slept on one, and his son and I on the other."[8]

The new industrial world seemed far from perfect to the growing working class, but it still offered much better opportunities than did the poverty-ridden villages from which they had come. Workers quickly oriented themselves and acted collectively to improve their lot. Strikes punctuated the cycle of industrial life.

Worker unrest was not dependent upon the consciousness-raising efforts of parties (Marxist or Populist); workers developed a spontaneous pro-

test movement on their own. There was, however, an important intermingling between urban factory workers and the radical intelligentsia. Workers confirmed the radicals' intellectual faith in Marxist analysis. Their very lives illustrated the degradation that the tsarist state visited upon its masses. The workers' rebellion was rooted in resentment, frustration, and anger at the bosses and authority figures who trampled their sense of elementary justice. Radical intellectuals injected revolutionary ideas into this atmosphere, further stirring the emotions of the already volatile masses. Their concepts and activities helped crystalize and accelerate the formation of a class consciousness among workers. This class consciousness kindled the workers' awareness that they belonged to a broad community different from and often antagonistic toward other social groups. Through a series of strike actions, workers gained a sense of their own power and ability to alter the status quo. They adopted revolutionary jargon to articulate political and personal goals. Marxist class terminology eloquently expressed the sense of social and political injustice they and other members of Russian society bitterly felt, and it became a common language of discourse as well as of protest.

Insurgent or oppositional activity was never easy in tsarist Russia. The government prohibited most public meetings. It forbade them even to those gentle men who headed the organs of local self-government and who were entrusted by Alexander II's great reforms with providing elementary education, medical care, road construction, and other ser-

■ n the 1890s many peasants
■ became metalworkers.

vices. When they and their brethren in the urban professions (doctors, lawyers, professors, journalists) wanted to nudge Russia prudently toward a more liberal, democratic system, modeled on England, they had to act surreptitiously. For everyone detesting the oppression of late nineteenth-century tsarism, clandestine activities became the norm, stealth the watchword.

THE FIRST REVOLUTION

As Russia entered the twentieth century, all the groups that had limned their political traits earlier and would soon emerge from the underground to form the country's political parties—the Marxists, the Populists, and the liberals, the main contenders for power in 1917—independently adopted similar organizational plans. Well adapted to the conditions of underground work, they each formed a small, elite, and secret central group to direct their most important activity: the publication of an illegal newspaper. Each group established a center abroad to print its oppositional paper (*The Spark, Revolutionary Russia,* and *Liberation,* respectively), to smuggle it back into Russia, and to distribute it throughout the country. The different approaches to fostering change found receptive audiences among the various parts of Russian society, which had grown remarkably strong within the context of a state structure that remained intransigent and backward.

In the early years of this century the Russian government appeared incapable of ameliorating the people's discontent. Indeed, its actions seemed only to exacerbate tension and increase alienation. Peasant rebellions occurred in several Ukrainian provinces and were ruthlessly suppressed. Students peacefully demonstrating for greater freedom suffered a bloody beating by Cossacks stationed in St. Petersburg. The official church, headed by K. P. Pobedonostsev, the tsar's childhood tutor and confidant, excommunicated the much-beloved novelist Leo Tolstoy. Strikers at factories, such as the Putilov steel factory in St. Petersburg, found themselves under siege by a police force with orders to crush their strike. Powerful police supervision became more evident and more ugly in factories throughout the country. At one mine in the Ural Mountains, troops slaughtered sixty-nine striking workers as they restored order. Agents provocateurs became more and more common in student and worker groups. Everyone risked arbitrary searches of person and home. One important bureaucrat boasted in 1904, "There is no citizen who can rest assured that his home won't be searched and he himself won't be arrested."[9] Government agents again instigated murderous pogroms against Jewish communities; government-inspired anti-Semitism, spread by the thuggish Black Hundreds, took on new life. The infamous 1903 Kishinev pogrom focused worldwide attention on retrograde tsarist policies. The revulsion engendered by this massacre was not the reaction the pogrom's instigators had counted on. One key minister had hoped that such Jew-baiting and Jew-beating would make Jews the scapegoat for the unpopularity of the regime. Thousands of Jews tried to flee abroad, many to America.

The actions of a few militant youths further distanced government figures from the realities of modern Russian life. Terrorism, an attack on autocracy through assassination, sprang up once again. Members of a special "fighting section" of the Socialist Revolutionary party, as well as a select group of anarchist bomb throwers, executed key government figures, including two ministers of the interior, members of the royal family, and provincial governors. One assassin explained: "We consider it not only our right, but our sacred duty, notwithstanding all the repulsion which such means of struggle inspires in us, to answer violence with violence and to pay for the spilt blood of the people with the blood of its oppressors. The crack of the bullet is the only possible means of talking with our ministers, until they learn to understand human speech and listen to the voice of the country."[10]

Into this early twentieth-century maelstrom of social and political tension the government threw a little attention-grabbing bomb of its own, a war in far-off Asia. As Vyacheslav Plehve, the minister of internal affairs, said, "In order to hold back the revolution, we need a small victorious war."[11] In January 1904 Russia went to war against Japan. For the tsarist regime the results proved disastrous, both at home and abroad. At first, nationalism, patriotism, and loyalty caused insurgents of all stripes to postpone their clashes with the state. But in short order, defeats and the incompetent management of the war empowered the opposition movement with new strength and, equally important, with a commonality of purpose.

Then in a single, mindless act, the government shattered the people's traditional faith in their monarch. Bloody Sunday, 9 January 1905, marked the violent start of the first Russian Revolution and touched off a ripple that would extend in the most profound way into 1917. On that bitterly cold Sunday morning, some two hundred thousand men and women followed an activist priest, who was employed by the government to divert workers' political discontents into "safe" economic concerns, into the square before the Winter Palace. Workers, their wives, and their children peacefully came to plead for a redress of their grievances before their supreme god on earth, the tsar. The workers, most of whom had joined a strike a few days before, carried icons, portraits of the tsar, and a petition:

> O sire! We working men of St. Petersburg, our wives and children, and our parents, helpless and aged men and women have come to you, our ruler, in quest of justice and protection. We are beggars, we are oppressed and overburdened with work; we are insulted, we are not regarded as human beings but are treated as slaves who must suffer their bitter lot in silence. We have suffered but are driven further and further into the abyss of poverty, injustice and ignorance; we are strangled by despotism and tyranny so that we can breathe no longer. We have no strength at all, O Sovereign. Our patience is at an end.[12]

Troops met the procession; shots were fired into the tightly packed mass. Cossacks bore down on the unarmed thousands. The unexpected attack paralyzed the petitioners at first, making them even easier targets. Then, as the dead and wounded fell, paralysis gave way to panic and stampeding. Soldiers pursued the fleeing thousands; innocent spectators shared the fate of the demonstrators. In the end, perhaps a thousand people died, as did faith in the tsar as a true defender of the Russian people's interests against the bureaucrats and the greedy self-interests of the upper classes. Immediately afterward, massive strikes gripped the capital and sympathy strikes flared up throughout the country. An immense, intensive politicization took hold of Russia.

Unity of purpose and unification of strengths became the dictum of all progressive Russians. A tacit popular front of all political groups, the All-Nation Struggle against Absolutism, pressed the government for fundamental reforms. Across a wide social spectrum, from meek university professors to radical locomotive drivers, men and women joined the public protest for the first time by enlisting in political-professional unions. These entities were in turn joined in a Union of Unions, which spearheaded the movement for change. It emphasized political, not social, revolution. Its members demanded political rights, human rights, and civil rights. Like the 1905 Revolution itself, the Union of Unions was a nonexclusive, nondoctrinaire group of men and women pledged to amorphous but widely held beliefs in a democratic system. The convocation of a Constituent Assembly, based on general, direct, equal, and secret elections without discrimination according to sex, religion, or nationality, and advocating a full program of civil liberties, stood as the keystone of this solid front against autocracy. Even the most timid liberals cast aside their ethical qualms about the use of violence to achieve change. They believed that all means must be tried to eliminate the "pirate gang" then in power.

Throughout the spring and summer of 1905, Russia's cities simmered with unrest. In Odessa, sailors mutinied on the battleship *Potemkin*. By the fall, society found a way to confront the state. In a general strike begun by the railwaymen's union in October, the broad liberationist coalition forced autocracy to grant new freedoms. Sergei Witte, the man who extricated the country from its unfortunate war with Japan, convinced the tsar to issue a special manifesto on 17 October, promising freedom of the press, of opinions, of assembly, and the creation of an elective legislative body, a Duma, to help conduct the nation's business. Moderates welcomed this limited parliament as an opportunity to bring about measured reforms through a regulated, Western European, nonsubversive political process.

Radicals found another way. They embraced the soviets of workers' deputies. A *soviet* was a spontaneously created "council" of men elected in factories. The St. Petersburg Soviet was the most famous, but there were soviets in many other cities, such as Moscow, Ivanovo, and Voznesensk, as well. These products of the labor movement, of worker self-government, proved to be a phenomenon of great brilliance and originality. The St. Petersburg Soviet of Workers' Deputies acquired a fiery young chairman, Leon Trotsky, a Menshevik, after its original leader was arrested. But as soon as the government regained its balance, Trotsky and the other members of the St. Petersburg Soviet found themselves in prison, too. The Moscow Soviet held out for greater economic concessions than its St. Petersburg counterpart. It called another general strike and by early December felt strong enough to stand at the center of an armed uprising against autocracy. With the peasants inactive, the government could concentrate all its forces on securing the rail line between the two capitals. Its loyal troops poured into Moscow and ruthlessly suppressed the rebellion. This was but the opening gambit in a punitive campaign waged across the country by rail. Military men moved methodically from place to place utilizing flogging parties and firing squads as the chief instruments of pacification. The working class suffered a stunning defeat in 1905. The bitterness engendered by the government's retaliatory missions endured, but so did the workers' taste of power and freedom and their memories of the soviets of workers' deputies.

Russia entered a period of semiconstitutionalism with high hopes for the Duma and continued anger about the lost Revolution. The country's first experiment with elections produced a body of Duma representatives radical in mood. The more than two hundred peasant deputies sided with others in the Duma who saw it as "an organ of struggle," a civilized forum in which to continue the movement

begun in 1905. These militant peasants stridently called for the dissolution of large noble estates and their sale, at cheap prices, along with state-owned land. Such stridency alarmed the tsar, who ordered the Duma dissolved. Elections to a Second Duma yielded even greater confrontations as more extreme leftists faced off against ultrarightists. After a short, heated life the Second Duma, too, fell victim to a dissolution order. A new prime minister, Stolypin, gerrymandered the electoral system, halving the number of peasant deputies and skewing membership in favor of wealthy nobles, priests, and rich merchants. Stolypin, whose new electoral system remained in place until 1917, explained that it was an effort "to pick and choose, bit by bit, from the Russian chaos those elements in which the feeling of loyalty to the regime still lived . . . to tear the State Duma from the hands of the revolutionaries . . . and to squeeze it into the system of state administration."[13] The Third Duma was a full-hearted reassertion of the regime's intransigence.

Between the elections to the Third Duma and the start of the world war political as well as social attitudes became increasingly polarized. The working class was at first depressed and chastened by its defeats in 1905 as well as by a subsequent economic downturn. The intellectuals and much of the intelligentsia had reacted in horror to the workers' spontaneous, radical activities during the Revolution. The specter of an urban *Pugachevshchina* now haunted them. Many felt that decades of self-sacrifice had brought about significant political reforms. Social usefulness had dominated their lives and their artistic expression. But several generations of obsession with revolution vanished once they faced its unvarnished realities. Soon a reckless, unlimited sensuousness replaced it. The postrevolutionary period was a time to make up for self-sacrifice with self-indulgence. Young people encouraged one another "to burn the candle at both ends." A huge gulf now separated workers and members of the intelligentsia; they lost their commonality of purpose. When a new generation of young workers, unschooled in the lessons of the failed Revolution, flocked to the cities during the industrial upswing just before the war, the social, psychological, and political cleavages dividing cities became even more pronounced.

The situation in the countryside was even more extreme. Nobles had feared for their lives during and after the 1905 Revolution. The most liberal among them were purged of their responsible positions as the nobility turned conservative and clung to privilege and autocracy. At no time since the Pugachev uprising had the monarchy and the nobility been so mutually interdependent. They feared the peasants and sought to control them, by repressive actions if necessary. One landowner explained: "Driven out of their senses by irresponsible agitation, the dark and uncultured mass, partly terrorized by their worst elements, have lost all concept of the basis of civil order. The desire to take what does not belong to them, to resolve economic questions by fire and violence, have awakened within the peasants distrust and hatred towards the people who have stood at the helm of [local self-government] for more than forty years."[14]

Peasants quickly lost faith in the Duma when it failed to deal with their desperate need for land. The government's attempt to foster individual farming units and allow small independent farmers to have a stake in the existing order of things at the expense of the commune proved half-hearted and ineffective. Thus, while the peasantry looked toward some apocalyptic future in which the whole old order would change, the landowners clung to the anachronistic, ossified structure of the old regime.

NICHOLAS THE LAST

The last great public event before the war was the celebration of the three hundredth anniversary of Romanov rule. Feasts, festivals, fancy balls, and state processionals, as well as the sale of trinkets, marked the occasion. Perhaps for the first time in his reign, certainly for the first time since the 1905 Revolution, Nicholas II rode on horseback (he was a superior horseman), unprotected, through the streets of Moscow, his wife and the royal children following in an open carriage. Those waiting for him at the Kremlin gates heaved an audible sigh of relief when he arrived safely. This act of bravado may have ended without incident, but it proved to

Tsar Nicholas II, Tsarina
■ Alexandra, and their firstborn, Olga, visiting their relatives, Queen Victoria and her son, the future Edward VII, in 1896.
BOTTOM

Nicholas and Alexandra
■ leading the grand celebration of the 300th anniversary of Romanov rule, 1913.

be an empty gesture: it did not signify any new thinking about the Russian people or politics on the part of Russia's last tsar, nor did it do anything to bridge the gulf separating the rulers from the ruled. The grand event failed to evoke mass sentiment for the tsar as the leader of the nation. It did not generate, as the most effective public ceremonies can, a collective effervescence that unites society.

Nicholas had not changed, but his country had. When he suddenly came to the throne after the premature death of his father in 1894, the first article of the Fundamental Law of the Empire held: "The emperor of all the Russias is the autocratic and unlimited monarch. God himself commands that his supreme power be obeyed out of conscience as well as fear." No other power stood above or in any way infringed on that of the autocrat. Upon accession to the throne Nicholas dismissed as "senseless dreams" the timid appeal of some liberal nobles that he "heed the voice of the people's need," i.e., consult with representatives of the organs of local self-government. "I . . . will maintain the principle of autocracy as firmly and inviolably as my unforgettable father," Nicholas insisted.[15] Even when circumstances, such as the establishment of the Duma in 1905, forced him to yield on this principle, the tsar maintained his backward-looking attitude. He developed the idea that the Duma was "primarily a platform for revolutionary propaganda."[16] Generally, Nicholas sought not solutions to problems but scapegoats. When not accusing advocates of change of being revolutionaries, he pointed his finger at

Wandering Russian pilgrims,
■ often called "holy fools."

other groups. He told a German ambassador that "international Jewry," in league with "demagogy" had been the driving forces of the 1905 Revolution. To another German ambassador, he claimed, in language echoing the "Judeo-Masonic" proclamations of the reactionary Pamyat (Memory) organization today, that the connections between Jews and Freemasons presented Russia with great dangers.[17]

Nicholas was trained to be dutiful; he had a strong sense of obligation and excelled at routine. Strict adherence to form and appearance often seemed more important to him than adherence to matters of substance and real power.

Just before the war a massive wave of strikes gripped St. Petersburg. More than 110,000 workers were out on strike there, as well as in the Baku oil fields and in other cities. Almost every factory in the workers' section of the city shut down. An elemental fury seized the workers, who fought in the streets with Cossacks and police. Barricades were built, bullets flew. The police reported that the workers had "gone berserk." Unlike 1905, while violence dominated the workers' world, in other parts of the city the good citizenry went on with its normal business. There was no solid or united front against autocracy. This lack of solidarity, of course, only encouraged working-class extremism, since it underscored the workers' sense of isolation and psychological distance from their better-dressed, one-time allies in the civil society. The violence unleashed in the workers' districts coincided with a more general crisis in the upper reaches of government as Nicholas considered returning to the pure autocracy of his father by reducing the Duma's role and replacing assertive ministers. Two crises—one from above, the other from below—put urban Russia on the brink of revolution early in the summer of 1914.

Even before the disorientation of the first Revolution, the tsar, who had little interest in the modernization of his political world, withdrew into his own idyll, the personal world of his family, well hidden in royal residences. One very close member of the court, Protopopov, wrote, "The characteristic feature of the Imperial family is their inaccessibility to the outside world and their atmosphere of mys-

Tsar Nicholas II and
■ Tsarevich Alexis.

RIGHT

The "holy devil,"
■ Grigory Rasputin.

ticism."[18] The mysticism was introduced by the tsarina, the German-born Princess Alexandra. Upon her conversion to Russian Orthodoxy, she embraced her new religion with the wholehearted enthusiasm of a convert. Her "Germanness," not an issue when she and Nicholas married in 1894, became a cause of concern and speculation when anti-German feelings exploded at the onset of the world war. Angry crowds sacked German stores, threw rocks at the German embassy, and intimidated German citizens. The government even changed the capital's name from the Germanic St. Petersburg to the more Russian Petrograd.

Once her hemophiliac son Alexis was born, Alexandra's frustrating search for a cure turned her strict religious observance into fanaticism. She sought out healers who exhibited an ability to ease the tsarevich's (heir apparent's) suffering. Alexandra acquired, as Nicholas had, a very Russian belief in the special spiritual and healing powers of wandering pilgrims. Sometimes these people, half-mad "holy fools" or "God's slaves," as they were called, spent their lives wandering around the country barefoot and in rags, even during the harsh Russian winters, living off charity as they performed simple miracles. Sometimes they lived as monks. Several of these revered outcasts were introduced into court circles, including the infamous Rasputin, a "man of God from Tobolsk Province [Siberia]." In the

decade before the Revolution, Rasputin's influence grew as the stresses on the family increased. The tsarina became dependent upon him, as her letters to him reveal: "How tedious I am without you. I breathe easily only when you, my teacher, sit beside me and I kiss your hand and put my head on your holy shoulder. Oh, how light I am then! I want only one thing—to sleep, to sleep an eternity on your shoulder. Oh what happiness just to feel your presence near me. When I hear you my head bows and I feel the touch of your hand."[19]

With Rasputin's backing, the tsarina encouraged the tsar's political intransigence. She believed he was too weak willed. To preserve the autocratic regime inherited from her father-in-law for her ailing son, Alexandra insisted that the tsar refuse to compromise. She wrote to him, "Forgive me, . . . but you know you are too kind and gentle . . . be more decided and sure of yourself—you know perfectly well what is right." She encouraged him to show no mercy to unsubmissive politicians, "Be Peter the Great, Ivan the Terrible, Emperor Paul; smash them all," or more pointedly: "You have never lost an opportunity to show your love and kindness; now let them feel your fist. They themselves ask for this— so many have recently said to me: 'We need the whip.' This is strange but such is the Slavonic nature—the greatest firmness, even cruelty and— warm love. They must learn to fear you; love alone is not enough." To the first of these inspirational messages, the tsar of the Russian Empire replied, "Tender thanks for the severe written scolding. Your poor little weak-willed hubby."[20]

At first, the war that saved Russia from another revolution in July 1914 united state and society. Oppositional activities were put on hold "for the duration." All but a few Bolshevik figures in the Duma pledged fealty to the national cause. Except for the most antiwar party members (Bolsheviks, Anarchists, some Mensheviks) and the reactionary Right, the political leaders formed a *union sacre,* a sacred union. As Pavel Miliukov, leader of the liberal Constitutional-Democratic (Kadet) party explained: "Our first duty is to preserve the unity and integrity of our country and to defend its position as a world power. . . . No matter what our attitude towards

Russian infantry at the front.

the government's domestic policy, our first duty is to preserve the unity and integrity of our country. . . . Let us not offer our adversary the slightest pretext for relying on the disagreements that divide us."[21] The war thus brought Russia the unity and the commonality of purpose that had been missing from the three hundredth anniversary of Romanov rule. But ironically, this "capital" of goodwill was soon to be squandered by the country's leaders.

The war began well enough. In a very orderly kind of *shturmovshchina*, the army, which numbered 1,423,000 men on 18 July 1914, managed to mobilize 3,915,000 additional men in two weeks. (During the entire war, 14,375,000 men were drafted, making a total of 15,798,000 men in uniform or about 37 percent of the adult male population.)[22] One famous writer, Konstantin Paustovsky, recalled a friend's reaction to seeing peasant soldiers marching through Moscow: "I walked right up to the front ranks to get a look. You know, they smell of bread. An amazing smell. You smell it and for some reason you believe that nobody can ever defeat the Russian people."[23] Soon, however, battles such as Tannenberg left millions dead or wounded. Defeat followed defeat; retreats followed defeats. In the first ten months of the war, officially reported casualties reached 3,880,000 men. The rightist patriot V. V. Shulgin, who selflessly left his sanctuary as Duma member and editor for army service, recalled, "We danced 'the last tango' on the rims of trenches filled with forgotten corpses."[24] The antiquated supply system could not keep up; the army's calculations

for shells and bullets were based on a quick series of victorious campaigns. Recruits were trained and sent to the front without weapons. Headquarters told commanders to arm them with weapons recovered on the battlefield. The new troops did not look or feel very much like soldiers. The slaughter of Russian boys continued. The war quickly turned into a great ordeal. One talented and honest general, Brusilov, said: "In a year of war the regular army had vanished. It was replaced by an army of ignoramuses."[25]

In 1915 Nicholas decided to remove Grand Duke Nikolai Nikolaevich as commander in chief of the army and assume the position himself. The grand duke, who was certainly grand in stature—he stood, like Peter the Great, close to seven feet tall—may not have been successful, but he was popular. One Russian diplomat explained: "The soldiers liked him and the public trusted him. He kept aloof from court intrigues and did not listen to suggestions of how the war should be conducted. A favorite story among the public was that when Rasputin once announced that he was coming to headquarters to speak with the grand duke, the latter had replied: 'If

Grand Duke Nikolai Nikolaevich (1856–1929).

you come, I'll hang you.' The story may not have been true, but it greatly increased the grand duke's popularity."[26]

Nicholas took over his experienced relative's post against the better judgment of his cabinet and most of his relatives. They were concerned not about his commanding the army but about who would govern the country and keep order in the capital in his absence. The tsar had his own plans, "Think, my wifey, will you not come to the assistance of your hubby now that he is absent?"[27] In other words, the tsar entrusted the tsarina with running the government while he was away at the front. As a Columbia University economics professor, who was a Russian army veteran of the period, put it: "After the middle of 1915 the fairly honorable and efficient group who formed the top of the bureaucratic pyramid degenerated into a rapidly changing succession of the appointees of Rasputin. It was an amazing, extravagant, and pitiful spectacle, and one without parallel in the history of civilized nations."[28] With Rasputin's advice, the tsarina dismissed ministers who exhibited the slightest degree of critical-mindedness. Sometimes she replaced officials on a whim, substituting a favorite for a competent man. One politician even coined the phrase "ministerial leapfrog" for this cabinet shuffle. The Russian ambassador in London, on being introduced to the man who turned out to be the last minister of the interior, commented, "C'est un imbecile."[29]

The shuffling of ministers alarmed many Russians, especially those in the capital who were concerned with politics and the faulty handling of the war. To many ordinary citizens it seemed that the German-born empress was deliberately sabotaging the government to help the enemy. The new men proved incapable, incompetent, and uncaring. They could do little to regulate the overtaxed railroad system. Refugees flooded back from the front areas. The rear could not supply the front, no less the cities. The strains caused by drafting men from villages weakened agriculture and, consequently, the food supply. Even the elite diplomatic corps had trouble obtaining provisions. The American ambassador's valet wrote home in September 1916: "They

Rasputin and a few of his "admirers."

have ordered a ship load of groceries from America and if it does arrive I think it will be the means of Saving a good many lives this Winter. I believe their [sic] will be more people starve to death here in Petrograd than they will kill with Bullets."[30]

The sullen, defeatist mood that began festering among the troops in 1915 spread to the civilian population. Rumors of Rasputin's debauchery compounded the conspiracy theories that were circulating about the tsarina. Soldiers interpreted Russia's series of retreats as a direct result of treason: "According to a majority of soldiers the chief culprits in the war were the Germans who came to Russia and picked off the best jobs in factories and industry. Even in the army they skimmed off the cream of the best jobs because the tsarina was German. But that wasn't enough for them, so they began a war to beat Russia for good." One officer, in an attempt to explain Russia's endless retreats to his soldiers, expressed the gist of popular thinking, "There are many spies and traitors in the high command, like the war minister, Sukhomlinov, who is to blame for the fact that we don't have any shells." To which a cook responded: "A fish begins to stink from the head. What kind of tsar is it who surrounds himself with thieves and chiselers?"[31]

Why did the Duma, chockablock with outspoken, if mostly moderate, critics of the government, do nothing? Duma members lacked an independent base. The tsar had dissolved the first two Dumas shortly after the first Revolution for their uncompromising radicalism and advocacy of sweeping land reforms. Moreover, he convened the Fourth, and last, Duma (formed just before the war) as little as possible, only to pass on needed appropriation bills. The moderates' dilemma was brilliantly presented by Vasily Maklakov's famous "mad chauffeur" parable, couched in thinly veiled Aesopian language to evade wartime censorship. The protagonist, the moderate centrist majority of the Duma (the so-called Progressive Bloc), is traveling by car over dangerous mountain roads. "He" is appalled to discover that his chauffeur, the government, drives so badly that he threatens all his passengers, the Russian people, with almost certain death. Maklakov describes the protagonist's quandary:

> What must you do? Force the chauffeur to vacate his seat? . . . This can't be done on a winding road in the mountains. He still has the wheel and drives the car—if you are not strong and skillful, one false move or hasty arm movement will crash the car. You know this and he knows it too and smiles at your fears and impotence. "Don't try to grab." He is right. You dare not try to grab the wheel. Perhaps fear or exasperation might lead you to forget the danger to yourself and make a grab for the wheel and risk a crash—but wait! It's not just yourself who is involved. Your mother is with you and your actions would kill her too. . . .
>
> So you restrain yourself. You postpone reckoning with the chauffeur until the danger passes and you are on level ground again. You let the chauffeur keep the wheel. More than this, you try not to get in the way, even helping with advice, directions, and cooperation. You are quite right—this is necessary.[32]

The best Duma members didn't necessarily huddle silently in fear, but neither did they provide alternative leadership.

Fall 1916 found even the reactionary right, so devotedly loyal to the throne, turned against the Siberian monk. The reptilian Duma member Purishkevich remarked, "All the evil comes from those dark forces, from those influences . . . which are headed by Grigory Rasputin."[33] In a lurid scene worthy of a horror movie, one of the tsar's young relatives, Prince Yusupov, entrapped Rasputin, murdered him, and dumped his body in the Neva river.

ON THE EVE

Soon after Rasputin's death, Russians celebrated the advent of the new year, 1917, in the midst of their third hard winter at war. Many keen observers of the European scene knew of the appalling toll the war was taking, but few anticipated that revolution would soon sweep through Russia. Lenin, living out the war in Switzerland, commemorated Bloody Sunday, 9 January, with a speech to Swiss youths:

> We must not be deceived by the present grave-like stillness in Europe. Europe is pregnant with revolution. The monstrous horror of the imperialist war, the suffering caused by the high cost of living everywhere engender a revolutionary mood; and the ruling classes, the bourgeoisie, and its servitors, the governments, are more and more moving into a blind alley from which they can never extricate themselves without tremendous upheavals. . . . We of the older generation may not live to see the decisive battles of this coming revolution.[34]

Prince Felix Yusupov and ■ his wife, Irina.
RIGHT
The tsar's daughters, Olga, ■ Tatyana, and Maria, in mourning for Rasputin.

Striking workers in
■ Petrograd, January 1917.

Events begun in a humble and unpretentious fashion soon led to a revolution that surprised every revolutionary. A socialist revolutionary noted, "The revolution struck like lightning from the sky . . . it was a great and joyful event, unexpected even by those of us who had been working toward it for many years and always waiting for it."[35]

In the workers' districts, across Petrograd from the Winter Palace, where the tsarina changed well-fed, incompetent ministers on a whim as often as she changed her fine silk underwear, women workers—many with husbands at the front—lived much less refined lives. The capriciousness of the bread supply governed their existence. Coping with more than 200 percent inflation, with the frustrations of lining up in the cold in front of bakeries that ran out of supplies too early, and with the constant struggle to find heating wood, wore these women down. Letters to and from the front revealed who was to blame: "The war is a matter of the hands and heads of clever people who hold power for their own selfish purposes." Inflation was seen as an intentional by-product of the war, which "fattens the rich and ruins the poor."[36] Rallies organized by women to commemorate International Women's Day (23 February, old style) quickly turned into demonstrations focused on the most essential needs of daily life. Crowds took to the streets demanding "Bread!" Things snowballed spontaneously. For instance, women workers at the Neva Thread Mills heard

chants from the streets. At first confused by the noise, they soon understood and began urging one another to quit work, shouting, "Into the streets! Stop! We've had it!"

It took little sophistication for those fed up with inequities to affix blame. Placards proclaiming DOWN WITH THE MONARCHY! appeared. No great pre-planning by experienced revolutionary leaders was needed; famous revolutionaries were sitting out the war in Siberian exile or abroad. No inspirational orators drew people into the streets; something more powerful—hunger and frustration—brought them out. Self-appointed neighborhood and factory leaders helped direct the people who were pouring out into the street. And because of the war, there were more people to mobilize. To meet the nation's defense requirements, the capital had become the hub of a sophisticated war industry. Since 1914 the working population had grown some 60 percent, largely in the ranks of skilled metalworkers. Unrest hung heavy in the workers' districts. They did not need outside agitators to help them understand the connection between their economic misery, the war, and high politics. All the revolutionary parties, who for decades had been plotting and planning, played little part. As one revolutionary (Mstislavsky) recalled, "The revolution caught us, the party people of those days, like the foolish virgins of the Bible, napping."[37] Such men may not have been virginal, but they were very much asleep at the switch.

In one of the many ironies that fill the history of 1917, it was the armed forces, sworn to uphold the tsar's regime, that made the crucial difference in February. In a worried report on 25 February the tsar's secret police noted, "Among the military units summoned for the purpose of suppressing the disorders, one may observe [cases of] fraternization with the demonstrators, and in some units even manifest approval, encouraging the mob by saying 'Press harder.'"[38]

Although early on some mounted police shot demonstrators, key troops, notably the Pavlovsky Regiment, sympathized more with the mobs making history than with the forces of law and order trying to restrain it. Ordinary soldiers were fed up too. They resented the gendarmes who looked military, but remained in Petrograd while rank-and-file soldiers went off to freeze and die at the front. The Pavlovsky Regiment mutinied; the Volynsky Guards refused to perform any police duties, then it, too, mutinied. Troops killed officers and declared themselves revolutionaries. They raided arsenals and armed the populace. The police could neither control nor intimidate the crowds with gunfire. "Ah-h Pharaohs!" one eyewitness reported the mob howling on a key thoroughfare, "Your end is coming."[39] The people, "the street," were in charge of the capital, not the government.

In a more substantive irony, one that established the underlying dynamic of authority from March to November, the workers' actions in the street would result in their social betters assuming power in a Provisional Government. At the same time, the workers swiftly reinstituted the Soviet of Workers' Deputies, the rough democratic institution that had been their great innovation of 1905. The bright image of workers' self-governance, of an elected council of representatives, had remained alive in the popular imagination of the Petersburg working class. Between 1905 and 1917 the revolutionary parties paid little attention to this innovation. After the war began, some parties considered reviving the idea of the soviet as a means of coordinating workers' movements, but little came of it. Once the strike movement deepened into revolution, however, the phrase "Soviet of Workers' Deputies" sprang from the lips of many socialist organizers and workers. People were heard screaming from lampposts: "Comrades, the time we were waiting for has finally come! The people have risen against their oppressors. Don't waste a minute! Create workers' district soviets! Draw representatives of the soldiers into them!"[40] Soon workers and soldiers alike were flocking to mass meetings of the Soviet of Workers' and Soldiers' Deputies.

Thus, two distinct sources of power, a widely divergent dual authority, emerged. The tsarist secret police, in its last insight, recognized the inherent divisiveness of this dual-authority arrangement, but failed to exploit it. In analyzing the danger posed by the workers' movement in February, they observed:

The situation is aggravated by the fact that the bourgeois circles also demand a change of government, so that the Government remains without any support whatsoever; however, in this instance, there is one favorable phenomenon: the bourgeois circles demand only a change of government and have taken the stand of continuing the war until its victorious conclusion, while the workers have advanced the slogans: "Bread," "Down with the Government," "Down with the war." This last point introduces [an element of] discord between the proletariat and the bourgeoisie, and only because of this are they unwilling to support each other. This difference of opinion represents a circumstance in favor of the Government, as it divides forces and pulverizes the initiative of the individual circles.[41]

The fact that a spontaneous uprising, a movement of "the street," overthrew the powerful tsarist regime upsets our mythical image of the Russian Revolution. With perfect hindsight, some party members would claim that they or their party led the February Revolution. Especially during the Stalin years, Party historians appropriated a leadership role for the Bolsheviks in February. Such claims don't stand up. As the best memoirist of the revolution, N. N. Sukhanov, explained:

> *There were no authoritative leaders on the spot* in any of the parties, almost without exception. They were in exile, in prison, or abroad. In the positions of the responsible heads of the great movement, at its most important moments, there were absolutely second-rate people, who may have been clever organizers but nevertheless were routine party hacks of the days of autocracy. It was impossible to expect of them, in the great majority of cases, a proper political perspective in the new situation or any real political guidance of events.[42]

The absence of first-rate leaders, an awareness that the massive military presence at the not-too-distant front might crush any revolution that "went too far," and a Marxist belief that a bourgeois regime would replace a feudal-autocratic one, deterred the revolutionary parties, through their representatives in the Soviet, from seizing the levers of governmental power. Moreover, subsequent events should not blind us to their anxieties and doubts about the Revolution's staying power. One leader of the Soviet recalled: "From minute to minute we expected that the [counterrevolutionary forces led by General Ivanov] would arrive, and if they did not shoot us they would take us away. . . . There was no certain conviction whatsoever in the success of the revolution."[43] However, the very existence of these second-rate leaders is an indication that the Revolution was not purely spontaneous. Some people, whose names are not well known to us, made a conscious attempt to transform unrest into a revolution against the old regime. They may not have been very well organized and they may never have had any power as a "temporary revolutionary government," but they did play an important role, as evidenced by the rallying of the insurgent masses around them. They succeeded, but they did not take over the instruments of state power.

The people making Petrograd's popular rebellion gave their mandate not to the "stuffed shirt" Duma politicians—men like Pavel Miliukov, "a creator of compromises . . . meant for quiet, normal times . . . not for times when irrational popular passions rage"[44]—but to men who they felt articulated their moods, aspirations, and views. They empowered people who they saw as their own leaders. The crowds making the Revolution trusted their own institutions. As the demonstrations gathered momentum, workers and soldiers—delegated by their respective factories, neighborhoods, or garrisons—as well as moderate socialist leaders, some just liberated from jail, others serving in the Duma, formed a provisional Executive Committee of the Petrograd Soviet of Workers' Deputies on 27 February. This self-appointed committee, composed at first of moderate socialists active in the workers' movements (primarily Mensheviks), helped bring the Soviet to life. Soon representatives from all of the revolutionary groups, including Bolsheviks, a variety of Men-

Menshevik N. S. Chkheidze (third from right), chairman of the Petrograd Soviet Executive Committee from February to September.

sheviks, Socialist Revolutionaries, and nonparty socialists, were elected to the Executive Committee. Membership changed as the composition of the Soviet changed, but the larger and more unwieldy the Soviet grew, the more responsible the Executive Committee became for carrying on the crucial political work. Several men served as chairmen of the Soviet, but N. S. Chkheidze, a Georgian Menshevik, sometimes called the "Papa of the Revolution," held the post from the end of February until Trotsky, riding a wave of Bolshevik popularity, took over in September. Sukhanov, a member of the Executive Committee, gave a good example of why the Committee had to act as the efficient arm of the larger Soviet. As the February Revolution unfolded:

> The Soviet was assembling. . . . The Duma White Hall was of course filled to overflowing. Instead of 700–800 deputies there were some 1,500 Workers' and Soldiers' Deputies . . . The Hall had never seen such an invasion or such people, "the sweepings of the streets," within its walls. Cigarette-ends were already scattered among the nice clean desks. Men sat in their caps and fur coats. There were glimpses here and there of rifles and other military equipment. The black figures of civilian workers were beginning to be submerged in the flood of grey army greatcoats. . . . Above this mass of human bodies . . . hung a thick cloud of smoke.[45]

The Tauride Palace, where the Duma met from 1906 to 1917.

BOTTOM LEFT

One of the last meetings of the Duma.

BOTTOM RIGHT

A meeting of the Soviet of Soldiers' Deputies in the Tauride Palace after the February Revolution.

A natural process, a kind of gravitational, popular democracy brought this mass together. They sought a nonbureaucratic way to give the city and the political movement direction, coordination, and organization. The hastily convened Soviet gave voice to popular aspirations; it gave the "gray," unprivileged people an institutional center.

From February to July 1917 the Petrograd Soviet met in the Tauride Palace, the same building that housed the Duma. It was "the brain and heart of the revolution."[46] While the quintessential representatives of "consciousness"—the pince-nez–wearing Duma members—were meeting in one wing, the representatives of "spontaneity"—the rough and ready deputies of the Petrograd working classes—were meeting in the other. An architect could not have constructed a more symbolic layout.

Duma representatives feared the spontaneity of "the street." Nevertheless, these specialists in beautiful parliamentary rhetoric considered themselves the country's brightest politicians. As the new year dawned they had sensed the approach of a thunderstorm of change and spoke out about the need to prevent it. Duma leaders still hoped the tsar would involve them in governance. Duma President Rodzyanko reflected in February: "I am not a rebel, I have made no revolution and do not intend to make one. If it is here, it is because they would not listen to us."[47] Only once the outcome of the unwanted Revolution became clear did these politicians, representatives of privilege, act. On 26 February the tsar ordered the Duma prorogued. The Duma obeyed. Some Duma members formed a private "temporary committee" to keep up with events.

This rump group of Duma members moved to organize a Provisional Government. It dispatched two monarchist members to receive the tsar's abdication in early March. Liberal party leader, Pavel Nikolaevich Miliukov, wanted to create a constitutional monarchy under the tsar's brother, Grand Duke Mikhail. But the new Provisional Government, with Miliukov as primus inter pares, could not guarantee the grand duke's life. He renounced the throne on 3 March, one day after the tsar's abdication. To the relief of many in the new government, the Romanov dynasty was at an end. Russia became a republic.

NEW REGIME—OLD PROBLEMS

Ten liberal ministers headed up the new nonpartisan regime vested with "the plenitude of power." This government did have the grace to call itself provisional. Its dominant personality, at first, was Foreign Minister Pavel Miliukov, a distinguished historian. He firmly believed that the laws of history dictated that nations followed an upwardly spiraling course of progress. For him, English parliamentarianism represented the ideal model. Sukhanov called him "the spirit and the backbone of all bourgeois political circles . . . head and shoulders above all his colleagues."[48] Miliukov stood above others not only because of his towering intellect but because of his great self-assured rationalism. He would not mold his beliefs to suit the fashions of the times. Thus, when he introduced the cabinet of the first Provisional Government to a boisterous session of the Soviet, he explained that the new premier, Lvov, was "the incarnation of Russian society oppressed by the Tsarist regime." From the crowd came shouts of "Propertied society!" whereupon Miliukov calmly explained, "Propertied society is the only organized society, which can enable other strata of Russian society to organize themselves too."[49] Miliukov recognized the deep social cleavages in Russia. Men like himself, he believed, could provide leadership, stability, and continuity while the "less developed" parts of society matured. He and his compatriots in the Provisional Government thought they spoke for national, not sectarian, interests, and

that they were best equipped to lead Russia in its development of a progressive, democratic, and Western European–like government.

Many others in the Provisional Government had played prominent roles in the All-Nation Struggle against Absolutism early in the century. They had been in the forefront of the fight for the establishment of liberal constitutionalism emphasizing civil rights for all. Those who belonged to the most potent liberal party, the Kadets, had used the Duma, over its twelve-year existence, as a national lectern from which to educate Russia about parliamentary government and rule of law. As professors to a nation of unenlightened pupils, they considered the inculcation of a democratic ethos as important as their ongoing fight for a democratic constitution. Not for nothing was the Kadet party nicknamed the "Professors" party (with all the stodginess, impracticality, and self-involvement the name implied). Others in and around the Provisional Government, notably Minister of Justice Alexander Fedorovich Kerensky, had gained national recognition for their involvement as defense attorneys in sensational political trials. In a series of causes célèbres, including the infamous Beillis trial (in which the government accused Mendel Beillis, a Kiev Jew, of murdering a young boy to obtain Christian blood for Jewish rituals), these Russian lawyers appeared as champions of the individual.

Not surprisingly, as soon as these paragons of civic courage assumed power they moved rapidly to implement political changes affecting individuals. Among the first acts on the Provisional Government's agenda was the abolishment of ranks and estates, the death penalty, censorship, and restrictions based on nationality or religion. They also established freedom of religion (and from religion), freedom of conscience and speech, of the press, and of movement, assembly, and domicile. The swift promulgation of equal rights for Jews made a deep and symbolically significant impression. The Romanov regime's blatant anti-Semitism—its prosecution of the Mendel Beillis case is but one example—had been abhorrent to Russia's most progressive citizenry. Equality for Jews became as important an issue to enlightened Russians as civil rights for blacks was to Americans in the 1960s. As the writer Maxim Gorky noted in his running newspaper column: "Equality for Jews is one of the wonderful achievements of our revolution. Having recognized the Jew to be equal to the Russian, we have removed a shameful, bloody and filthy stain from our conscience."[50]

"Equality for Jews," a rallying cry since 1905, was quickly made real by the February Revolution. Ironically, however, a revolution begun by ordinary women made no place for them or their parallel demand for equal rights, which also dated back to the first Revolution. Women benefited from changes in divorce and property laws, but nothing was said about their right to participate in elections. In March they began pressing for the vote in demonstrations down Petrograd's main thoroughfare, Nevsky Prospect. The throngs, including what the press called "Amazons on Horseback," brought to mind the great marches of the English suffragettes. The Russian feminists soon proved much more successful than their British sisters: they earned goodwill and the right to vote.

Russia's powerful working classes, too, gained much, both directly and indirectly, from February. As citizens of a new republic they attained a panoply of rights. They were now more enfranchised than their English, French, or German proletarian brothers: they were granted the right to strike (in wartime!); they had collective representation against management through their factory committees; their representatives in the Soviet of Workers' and Soldiers' Deputies gave them a voice in politics and in power, or more precisely, in dual power. Moreover, the general political amnesty that would soon free their socialist—Bolshevik, Menshevik, and Socialist Revolutionary—and anarchist heroes, leaders, and mentors, would provide them with first-rate leadership as these men came back from exile (from deep in Siberia to deep in the Bronx).

However, February's political revolution was not accompanied by a social revolution. The factories continued to run for the benefit of their capitalist owners. Workers struggled throughout the spring and summer for the democratization of factory life: an eight-hour day, better wages, and workers' control (monitoring management to insure that workers'

interests were protected). Although some members of the Provisional Government spoke out in favor of social reforms, they did so primarily to increase worker productivity for the war effort and to avoid social revolution by co-opting working-class militants. Questions of social justice and social change, paramount in importance to the left-wing parties as well as to other people who saw the soviets as the best representative of their interests, were not addressed. Instead, problems of fundamental social restructuring were assigned to be resolved by a Constituent Assembly. The convocation of this assembly, its delegates elected by universal, direct, equal, and secret voting procedures, to lay the foundation for a democratic, free Russia, had been a rallying cry of all progressive Russians since 1905. The Provisional Government promised the earliest possible meeting of the Constituent Assembly.

The Constituent Assembly, it was thought, would guarantee Russia's radiant future. Meanwhile, the hard realities of governance dictated that the government and the Soviet find ways of working together to defend the Revolution and the state. The strikes' disruption of the system of supplying materiel and provisions to the troops had to be resolved, and at the same time workers' grievances had to be ameliorated. In more general terms, a society that had been constricted by externalized—and over-

Women demonstrating for
■ the right to vote on
Nevsky Prospect, Petrograd,
March 1917.

bearing—authority now had to adjust to the chaos of internalized freedom. People who had little experience with moderation or compromise, not to mention open, mass, democratic political life, now had to adapt to it. Maxim Gorky addressed the issue: "We must understand, it is time for us to understand that the most dreadful enemy of freedom and justice is within us; it is our stupidity, our cruelty, and all that chaos of dark, anarchistic feelings, that chaos which has been cultivated in our souls by the monarchy's shameless oppression, by its cynical cruelty."[51]

Such philosophical reflections carried little weight with many of the workers and soldiers who made the February Revolution. Their goodwill toward the new regime insured tranquillity at first, as the French journalist Claude Anet saw reflected in the changing mix of banners and placards carried down the capital's main streets after February:

> Only a week ago, the following inscriptions dominated: "Long live the Democratic Republic; Land and Liberty; Long Live the Council of Workmen's and Soldiers' Delegates." These placards had not disappeared, but I saw with pleasure a great number on which I read: "Be United"; "Have Confidence in the Provisional Government and the Council of Workmen's and Soldiers' Delegates"; "Workmen, work for the defense of the Nation; Do not forget our brothers in the trenches; War until final Victory is achieved"; and this one, which in a lapidary form, gave the programme necessary at the present hour: "Workmen to the factories; soldiers, to the front."[52]

In the muddy, rapidly warming Russian spring, the exigencies of daily life reasserted themselves. The degree of patience or tolerance that the radical workers had for leaders preoccupied solely with questions of liberal, constitutional governance determined the dynamic and pace of further revolution in 1917. It was not merely a matter of which rights were more important, political or social. How long would Russia's "gray" masses continue to

"**L**ong Live the Democratic Republic! ■ Long Live the International!" a banner of the Rogozhsky Regional Soviet proclaims.

BOTTOM

Soldiers carrying a banner ■ that reads: "Greetings to Our Comrades in the Trenches."

endure the old order once they knew they could escape from their past burdens?

The new Provisional Government needed to act pragmatically. It had to decide which legacies from Romanov rule were the most egregious, which continuities of the previous regime—policies, procedures, or politics—would be the greatest source of tension to the radical workers. It needed to set priorities for its actions. Moreover—and most difficult for a group of men ruled more by intellect and proper procedure than by intuition or natural rhythms—the Provisional Government had to de-

Workers and soldiers
■ demonstrating against
the imperialist policies
of "Miliukov-Dardanelsky,"
April 1917.

velop keen timing to purge the country of the despised inheritances from the old regime.

Foreign policy continuities provided the most immediate source of conflict. This most traditional area of governance provoked the first crisis that shook, and then shook out, the Provisional Government. The tsarist secret police had discerned the antithetical positions that the two sides of dual power held on the war and had recommended exploiting these conflicting views during its very last days. Petrograd workers saw this clash not only as a policy and institutional dispute, but as an issue rooted in class conflict. As the general assembly of one large factory noted: 'The people and army went into the streets not simply to replace one government with another, but to carry out our slogans. These slogans are: 'Freedom,' 'Equality,' 'Land and Liberty' and 'An End to the Bloody War'—for us, the unpropertied classes, the bloody slaughter is not necessary."[53]

In 1917 the key to free, democratic Russia's foreign policy was the war, as it had been for the tsarist government. Just as the outbreak of the war had aroused patriotic enthusiasm, the destruction of the hated, incompetent regime responsible for countless deaths provoked a new outpouring of national pride and renewed devotion to the war. Popular behavior vividly mirrored this mood. Soldiers daring to desert were beaten and physically driven back to the

front by peasants. Many believed that new men would lead them to victory instead of to the cemeteries. A renewed fighting spirit emboldened millions of uniformed Russians and the Provisional Government quickly ordered the decks cleared for victory. But what were they fighting for?

The Provisional Government gained goodwill by pledging to defend the nation's supreme interests and to continue the war until victory. The Petrograd Soviet supported this pledge. But each side wanted a different kind of victory. The liberal government set as its goal "war to complete victory," a victory that would guarantee and extend Russia's power and territory. In this way the Provisional Government carried on a long-standing aim of tsarist foreign policy: control over the Dardanelles and acquisition of Constantinople. The historian's sweeping vision came into play here, as did his emotions and identifications. Miliukov, whose beloved son had died at the front, stood foursquare behind war until victory. For him, living up to treaty obligations with England and France put Russia in the position of fighting shoulder to shoulder with "the other great democracies," those parliamentary governments and centers of refined European culture he so admired.

The Soviet's goal directly contradicted that of the government. Led by moderate socialists, the Soviet believed in fighting "to defend the revolution" and to achieve a peace "without annexations and indemnities." The Soviet tried to foist these formulations on the Provisional Government, but Foreign Minister Miliukov rejected them as naive and serving the German cause. He continued to assert Russia's right to the long-desired foreign territories. When he informed Russia's allies, England and France, that the Provisional Government would observe all of its country's treaty obligations, including the secret treaties that promised the Turkish territories—most notably the Dardanelles, the gateway to the Black Sea—as a prize, he provoked a fire storm of protest known as the April Crisis. The incensed masses took to the streets to demonstrate against the tsarist war program of "Miliukov-Dardanelsky."

The demonstrations underscored not only the widely differing goals of foreign policy, but also the diverging conceptions of the purpose of the Revolution. They were the first open manifestation of the "we-they" gulf between the rulers and the ruled, at least in the capital. Reporters for a workers' newspaper saw these demonstrations as an explicit expression of class conflict: "Petrograd reacts unusually sensitively and nervously to the burning political issues of the day. Miliukov's note, published yesterday, called forth great agitation on the streets. Everywhere groups of people, meetings, which have of late become usual sights, but in immeasurably larger numbers. Everywhere, at street meetings, in trams, passionate, heated disputes over the war take place. The caps and handkerchiefs stand for peace; the derbies and the bonnets—for war."[54]

The protests reminded the government of how much it owed to the power of "the street." Miliukov, the focus of popular protest, was sacrificed to the god of civil peace by his liberal brethren. The Provisional Government was recast as a coalition. Moderate socialists were invited in as a way of calming "the street" and limiting further polarization. The clash between the popular and elite approaches to the war revealed the fundamental instability of the dual-power arrangement. It squandered the capital of goodwill that the Provisional Government had received as a birthright and signaled the trouble that the new government would have juggling continuities during a time of great change.

KERENSKY VS. LENIN

April brought more than just the first crisis to the new Russia. It threw a glaring spotlight on three political personalities: Miliukov, Kerensky, and Lenin. These were the men who made—or unmade—the revolutions of 1917.

Once Miliukov exited the government, Kerensky became the dominant figure. A socialist of slippery affiliation (he always believed in himself more than in any party structure), Kerensky was the only man to come into the first Provisional Government from the Soviet side; he had been a prominent member of the Petrograd Soviet's Executive Committee. Only thirty-six at the time of the Revolution, Kerensky differed markedly from most prominent Russian politicians. He lacked an accumulation of

French Minister of Munitions Albert Thomas (center) joins Kerensky (right) and General Lavr Kornilov (left) in a military parade.

scholarly or ideological publications. He was not highly organized or disciplined, nor did he have the *Sitzfleisch* for thorough, rigorous, political analysis. Relentless logic was far from his forte; Kerensky was not a skilled wordsmith whose pen turned out articles that changed people's thinking or reordered their lives. He rose above mediocrity with his marked gift for emotionally charged speechmaking. Famous for his work as a defense attorney in a series of celebrated political trials, Alexander Fedorovich, to use his Russian appellation, gained renown as a powerful oppositional orator in the last two Dumas. He enjoyed immense popularity in Petrograd, especially among the urban workers, who needed a popular spokesman during the war when the Bolshevik members of the Duma had been arrested and exiled.

Kerensky was an inspirational speaker and a great persuader. In person he had a fiery presence, matinee-idol good looks, and a booming, emotional delivery, all of which made a deep, if not particularly long-lasting, impression on his listeners. Albert Thomas, the French minister of munitions, accompanied Kerensky, who was named minister of war after the April crisis (earlier he had been minister of justice and was responsible for abolishing the death penalty), on his rounds as he rallied the troops. Thomas's analysis of his hero's oratorical powers explains the effectiveness of a Kerensky speech: "It is composed of appeals to sentimentality. He gives his whole heart to it. He naively adds all his thoughts, his very own sentimentality. This allows him to descend into the sentimentality of others. . . . There is charm and grace in his eloquence. He exuded faith in Russia, the revolution, a just peace and even a successful offensive."[55]

The "golden boy" of the Provisional Government was masterful at arousing passions. One eyewitness recalled: "When he left, they carried him on their shoulders to his car. They kissed him, his uniform, his car, the ground on which he walked. Many of them were on their knees praying; others were weeping. Some of them were cheering; others singing patriotic songs."[56] Women, especially middle-class and, as the year progressed, noble women, who increasingly saw him as the only bulwark against the "zoological anarchy" of the masses, went into hysterical fits over him. A Kerensky speech in a theater usually ended with a shower of buttons torn from blouses and rose petals. A British diplomat saw him speak at Moscow's Bolshoi Theater in June:

> When he stated that he was ready to die for the Russia of his ideals, there was no need of words to convince the audience of the sincerity of the man. . . . And when the end came, the huge crowd rose to greet him like one man. Men and women embraced each other in a hysteria of enthusiasm. Old generals and young praporshicks [sic] wept together over the man who all Russia feels can save the country from ruin. Women gave presents of jewelry, officers sacrificed their orders. An autographed photogravure of M. Kerensky was sold for 16,000 rubles and the whole theatre rained roses.[57]

The trouble with Kerensky's appeal was that it had no staying power. Once he left the scene there was no brilliant, trenchant political tract, newspaper, or leaflet to keep alive the impact of his oral persuasion. In revolutionary Russia the most persuasively powerful men, notably Lenin and Trotsky, combined superior speaking skills with brilliant pens. The ability to turn a fine phrase, especially in a neat, pithy slogan, mattered very much. Moreover, Kerensky's calls "to defend our young free-doms" soon wore thin as the social reforms the masses cared about did not materialize. To make matters worse, Kerensky's incipient egoism and vanity soon blossomed into an all too unsubtle Napoleon complex. During the summer he moved into the Winter Palace, slept in the tsar's bed, had himself photographed at the tsar's sprawling desk and in Napoleonic poses. Sukhanov, a longtime acquaintance but never a friend, noted: "He was a Socialist and a democrat . . . by conviction, taste, and temperament he was the consummate middle-class radical. But he believed in his providential mission to such an extent that he could not separate his own career from the fate of the contemporary democratic movement in Russia. This was why Kerensky saw himself not only as a Socialist but also as a little bit of a Bonaparte."[58]

Such vanity, combined with Kerensky's maladroit politics, exacerbated the gulf separating Russian society and government.

April brought Russia's most powerful revolutionary thinker, V. I. Lenin, back home from exile in Switzerland. It was intellect, not emotion that generated the power of his speeches. He did not inspire men—he convinced them. Sukhanov explained: "Lenin was in general a very good orator—not an orator of the consummate, rounded phrase, or of the luminous image, or of absorbing pathos, or of the pointed witticism, but an orator of enormous impact and power, breaking down complicated systems into the simplest and most generally accessible

Lenin addressing the
■ Petrograd Soviet
in the Tauride Palace,
April 1917.

elements and hammering, hammering, hammering them into the heads of his audience until he took them captive."[59]

After traveling through Germany in a sealed train, Lenin crossed the Baltic Sea to Stockholm and arrived in Petrograd at Finland Station—as so many returning revolutionaries did—to a tumultuous welcome. The brilliant leader of the Bolshevik party came back confident, as he had been for many years, that a socialist revolution was about to take place in Russia and that he and his party would lead it. Lenin returned not to praise the Provisional Government nor even to support the socialist Soviet of Workers Deputies, but to condemn them and his fellow Bolsheviks (Stalin, Molotov, and others) who supported dual power, and to push his party into active opposition. Niceties of reform did not interest him, issues of power did. The attainment of state power preoccupied his coolly analytical mind.

Lenin's arsenal of ideas was impressive. Gorky put it succinctly, "Lenin was a man who prevented people from leading their accustomed lives as no one before him was able to do."[60] Ever since the early years of the Russian Marxist movement, he had worked single-mindedly to forge an effective revolutionary party. A master of doctrine and arcane points of Russian Marxist analysis, Lenin was first and foremost a practitioner of revolutionary *realpolitik*. Nothing, not even friendship, took precedence. His friendship with Julius Martov, for example, the humanistic, highly intellectual leader of what became the Menshevik party, ended at the 1903 Russian Social Democratic Labor party congress when Lenin led the Bolsheviks against him over the issue of rules for party membership. Lenin argued for a "hard" position, a party consisting exclusively of professional revolutionaries, against Martov's "softer" approach.

Equally as impressive as Lenin's ideology was his power to communicate it and to act as a charismatic leader imparting new ways of thinking, new devotion and dedication to the Bolshevik cause. His magnetism was so strong that it made pre-1917 Bolshevism—before an open admissions policy took in tens of thousands of fresh recruits—very much a leader-centered movement. One of Lenin's collaborators, who subsequently became a Menshevik leader and firm enemy, A. N. Potresov, crisply dissected Lenin's charismatic quality:

No one could so fire others with his plans, no one could so impose his will and conquer by force of his personality as this seemingly ordinary and somewhat coarse man who lacked any obvious sources of charm. . . . Neither Plekhanov [the father of Russian Marxism] nor Martov nor anyone else possessed the secret radiating from Lenin of positively hypnotic effect upon people—I would even say, domination of them. Plekhanov was treated with deference, Martov was loved, but Lenin alone was followed unhesitatingly as the only indisputable leader. For only Lenin represented that rare phenomenon, especially rare in Russia, a man of iron will and indomitable energy who combines fanatical faith in the movement, the cause, with no less faith in himself. If the French king Louis XIV could say L'état, c'est moi, Lenin, without putting it into words, always had the feeling, Le parti, c'est moi, that in him the will of the movement was concentrated in one man. And he acted accordingly. I recall that Lenin's sense of mission to be the leader at one time made an impression upon me also.[61]

Well before he arrived back home Lenin besieged his followers from abroad, pressing them to take a harder line with the Provisional Government, to castigate it, and not to cooperate with it because it failed to deal with the burning issue of making peace. He urged radicals to concentrate not on some abstract future to be created by a Constituent Assembly, but on the essential question of power: "The basic question of every revolution is that of state power."[62] Once back in Petrograd Lenin threw a bombshell into Bolshevik policies and strategies with his "April Theses." From Bolshevik party headquarters in the Kshesinskaya mansion—a wonderful modern house commandeered by Bolsheviks from its owner, the ballet star and former special friend of Nicholas II—Lenin thundered against the party's conventional wisdom. In speeches and in the party newspaper, *Pravda*, he demanded withdrawal of all support for the Provisional Government; an end to the war; abolition of the police, the army, and the bureaucracy; nationalization of all land; and creation of a republic of soviets.

WHOSE WAR IS IT?

Lenin's forceful assault on the new status quo contrasted sharply with the painfully correct and deliberate approach of the Provisional Government. Not willing to prejudge fundamental social questions before a Constituent Assembly met, it seemed to be acting more as an interregnum than as a new regime. Moreover, once socialists from the Soviet entered the government, it was doubly handcuffed; it contained men believing in incompatible economic and social systems as well as men from the Soviet's different parties who, to further complicate matters, sometimes opposed one another on the great question of the war. (For instance, the much-beloved Socialist Revolutionary leader Viktor Chernov served as minister of agriculture during the summer, but could not promulgate his radical program for massive land redistribution because it struck liberals as presenting the Constituent Assembly with a *fait accompli* and because he was isolated from fellow socialists in the coalition government who disdained his anti-war stance.)

The Provisional Government's socialist members compromised their appeal by participating in an

Viktor Chernov, Socialist
■ Revolutionary party leader.

entity that workers, soldiers, and peasants increasingly saw more as a caretaker for the old order than as a creator of a new world. This disillusionment with the Mensheviks and Socialist Revolutionaries, whom the masses had considered to be their natural leaders, benefited the radical parties, particularly the Bolsheviks. The Georgian Menshevik leader I. G. Tsereteli foresaw this consequence on the eve of his entrance into the first coalition government: "If by entering the government we arouse in the masses expectations we are unable to satisfy, we strengthen the left, the maximalist tendencies. Then, besides weakening our influence over the masses we lose our capacity to influence the government, regardless of the presence in it of our representatives. *The disparity between the policies of the government and popular expectations will grow, and instead of strengthening democratic power, the result will be the strengthening of the maximalist sentiment of the masses.*"[63] Tsereteli's insight quickly proved prophetic, and there was nothing he and the Mensheviks could do about it.

Nowhere were the missteps of the Provisional Government more clearly manifested than in the armed forces. And nowhere were the results of the revolutionary process—the formation within the military of institutions and goals that differed from those of its traditional leadership—more evident. Although the men at the front drew strength from their belief that they had the power to change things, they initially pledged themselves to the patriotic "war to victory" theme so harmoniously sounded by the Provisional Government. Yet with every indication of the government's weakness or continued disorganization, the soldiers' impatience, already worn thin by years of staring across barbed wire at the enemy, intensified. Soldiers garrisoned in Petrograd had been key players in the February Revolution. Their great mutiny made repression impossible. Assisted by radical lawyers in the Petrograd Soviet they penned the famous Order No. 1, which was issued on 1 March. This document, a veritable constitution for the millions of men in uniform—primarily peasants—established the principle of forming committees of representatives elected from the rank and file. These committees, in turn, had representation in the Soviets of Workers' and Soldiers' Deputies, which monitored the government's military actions. In this way, democracy penetrated into the military. Significantly, Order No. 1 dissolved the regimented inequalities of the old order: honorary titles disappeared; rank lost its meaning; rudeness of superiors toward inferiors was banished. A dismantling of the hierarchical order of authority had begun.

The creation of soldiers' committees introduced a dual-command structure into the armed forces that mirrored the dual-power arrangement of the capital—a shaky coexistence of two institutions representing different social layers with different aspirations and priorities. Patriotism prompted soldiers to fight on. Charismatic speakers could inspire the troops to continue their efforts. But as the revolutionary soldiers became more confident, more accustomed to following their own instincts, as the war effort continued to stumble along without noted successes, their will to fight began to crumble.

Kerensky tried to rekindle a spirit of national unity. He sped from unit to unit at the front. He barnstormed, inspiring the troops to fight on in defense of freedom and the Revolution. "Warriors!" he addressed the men in the trenches: "The Fatherland is in danger. Freedom is threatened, the Revolution stands before the abyss! Your Supreme Commander [General Brusilov], beloved through victory, is convinced that each day of delay merely helps the enemy, and that only by an immediate and determined blow can we disrupt his plan. . . . in the name of its free people and its Provisional Government, I call upon the armies . . . to take the offensive. . . . Forward!"[64] Elsewhere he spoke to the troops from his automobile: "Having thrown off the chains of slavery of the tsarist power, the Russian people have become the freest people in the world. The people are now fighting for the happiness and freedom of the broad, working masses, for land and freedom, for the honor, independence, and dignity of the great free Russian people. Fighting in the name of the right to live freely, you are carrying, on the points of your bayonets, a message of the brotherhood of all peoples, of the triumph of the great principles of freedom, equality, and fraternity."[65]

But Kerensky's summer offensive stalled. It cost

Alexander Kerensky rallying ■ the troops at the front, June 1917.
BOTTOM

His inspirational speeches ■ boost soldier morale.

many lives, accomplished nothing, and only exacerbated the soldiers' disaffection. Some soldiers, perhaps under the influence of Bolshevik agitators, refused orders and engaged in open fraternization with enemy troops (much as Lenin had suggested in his "April Theses"). The Bolsheviks' newspaper, *Soldiers' Pravda*, which featured articles such as "Whose War is It?" "On Fraternization," "The Fight for Land," and a great gripe column, "Voices from the Trenches," was amazingly popular. Kerensky's sentimental appeals lost their power as soldiers more and more often retorted, "What good is land and freedom to me if I'm dead?"[66]

Failures at the front only magnified the Provisional Government's tragic flaw, its inability to shake off the tar baby of war and institute social reforms meaningful to the average man. To calm army traditionalists who claimed that such reforms as the abolition of the death penalty and the abandonment of censorship were undercutting officers' authority, a strict regime was instituted, replacing the liberalization of the spring. Those guilty of advocating disobedience to military orders were now to be punished as traitors. A strict disciplinarian and avowed enemy of soviets and Bolsheviks alike, General Lavr Kornilov, was made commander in chief. His actions would offend the urban working classes, the one group leaning toward the Bolsheviks and other radical parties without any help from the incompetence of the Provisional Government.

Already alienated from the propertied class before 1917, workers saw a gulf separating their interests from those of the Provisional Government long before their brothers in the villages or in the army did. The living school of revolution at which they studied throughout 1917 only increased their radicalism. They were responsible for setting and keeping in motion the flywheel of social and political change. Central to their escalating militancy was their assertion of control over their lives through their own working-class institutions, the Soviets of Workers' Deputies. Almost as important was their growing antagonism, rooted largely in class antipathy, toward the other extremely active urban group, the intelligentsia.

Ironically, the rich popular culture of the urban workers' world shared common values with the sophisticated, Europeanized world of the intelligentsia. This went deeper than the obvious sartorial imitation of high culture evident in pictures of workers decked out in their Sunday best. Like the intelligentsia, workers held sacred the achievements, or near achievements, of the 1905 Revolution. Every day, in their industrial ghettos, such as Petrograd's Vyborg district, on their way from vermin-infested domiciles to grimy factories, they passed corners where troops had shot workers or where bloody demonstrations had taken place. Such reminders of the old order, of old scores, and of old wounds were everywhere. They, too, believed in equality, justice, and democratic procedures, although their understanding of these concepts was based more on their own experiences and on socialist precepts than on foreign models.

Workers' insistent demands for social reforms after February finally began to be heeded in the spring, when many of them, particularly in Petrograd, obtained considerable raises. However, administrative confusion within the Provisional Government, transportation problems, the disconnection of the agricultural periphery from the urban-industrial centers, and more war-born inflation offset the wage gains. As the weather turned warm, factory workers felt little better off economically than they had during the cold winter days of February.

THE STREET WILL ORGANIZE US!

In June the radical workers' and soldiers' festering class antagonism came out into the open. The Provisional Government itself triggered the outbreak when its troops raided the Durnovo villa, a mansion that had belonged to P. P. Durnov, the governor of Moscow during the 1905 Revolution. Anarchists had "expropriated" the property in the wake of the February Revolution and set up their party headquarters in it. Several workers' organizations from the nearby soot-filled factory district were housed there and it became a popular center for workers' social, recreational, and political activities, until early June, when the anarchists tried unsuccessfully to seize another property, the newspaper *Russkaya volya* (Russian Liberty). The government felt it had to teach the radicals a lesson and restore property rights. During its assault on this fortress of radical activity one anarchist was killed in a shower of bullets. Seventy others were arrested, including activists from an important factory located next door. The government's prerevolutionary, gendarme-like, oppressive actions provoked a protest strike by the entire Vyborg (working-class) district that set the mood for June. A mass march organized by the First All-Russian Congress of Soviets of Workers' and Soldiers' Deputies—delegates from the thousands of soviets that had sprung up after February all over the country, "like mushrooms after a rain," as Russians would say—brought more than four hundred thousand representatives of Petrograd's factories and regiments out into the street. Their banners demanded the removal of the "ten capitalist ministers" in the Provisional Government, an end to the summer offensive, and a transfer of all power from the government to the Soviet.

Fed up with the inaction of the moderate socialist leaders in the Soviet, workers tried to push them to take power. Nothing exemplifies the pent-up frustration of the crowds in late June and early July better than the angry words hurled at SR leader and Minister of Agriculture Viktor Chernov when a group from Kronstadt grabbed him outside the Tauride Palace. "Take power, you son of a bitch, when it's given to you!" Only the appearance of Trotsky from inside the palace calmed the surging, heavily armed crowd and secured the release of this widely respected socialist.[67]

Another incident illustrating the workers' rage occurred during a session of the Soviet's Executive Committee in July. A worker from the giant Putilov Factory jumped onto the speaker's platform, rifle in hand, exclaiming:

> "Comrades! Must we workers endure such treachery much longer? You have gathered here where you make deals with the bourgeoisie and the landowners. You are betraying the working class. The working class will not stand for this. We Putilovites are 30,000 strong. We will get what we want. Absolutely no bourgeoisie! All power to the Soviets! We have our rifles tightly in hand. Your Kerenskys and Tseretelis won't vanquish us!"[68]

In early July, after the June offensive turned into another bloody disaster, restless soldiers staged a garrison mutiny. Gorky described the soldiers' actions as "disgusting scenes of madness." On 4 July he reported, "a truck flashes by like a mad hog; it is tightly packed with motley members of the 'revolutionary army.' Among them stands a disheveled youth who shouts hysterically: 'The social revolution, comrades!'"[69] Soldiers and sailors, many of whom had joined the Bolshevik party in the spring (in Petrograd alone its membership doubled from sixteen thousand to thirty-two thousand between April and June), and others who simply had been taken with highly effective Bolshevik and anarchist

propaganda calling for an end to the war and "All Power to the Soviets!" insisted that the Provisional Government be overthrown. To a certain extent, the rising mood of rebellion that marked the July days was the result of months of powerful Bolshevik propaganda against the government and agitation by rank-and-file party men in the factories. Lenin and the Bolshevik party leadership may thus have inspired the July days, but Lenin himself did not lead them. In fact, he played a moderating role. Remembering well the failures of 1905, he tried to temper the rebellious mood until it could be supported in the countryside and at the front. He feared that a premature uprising could destroy everything he had been working toward. Speaking to a heavily armed throng of Kronstadt soldiers from the balcony of Bolshevik headquarters at the Kshesinskaya mansion on 4 July, Lenin called for "peaceful" demonstrations, self-restraint, and vigilance, because he knew that the slogan "All Power

"**A**ll power to the Soviet! ■ Down with the Capitalist Ministers! Down with the State Duma!"

RIGHT

The writer Maxim Gorky ■ (1868–1936) in 1917.

to the Soviets!" would eventually triumph. It was his last public speech until October. Just a few days later, with no hope of victory in sight, Lenin was forced to retract the slogan and beat an ignominious retreat.

The July days were clearly an instance when the mood of the masses was far ahead of revolutionary learning and leadership. Extreme radicals, anarcho-communists, and highly politicized soldiers and sailors, including the first machine-gun regiment and men from the nearby Kronstadt navy base, had screamed for an overthrow of the government by armed force. The men rushing around, in Gorky's phrase, "like mad hogs," had no plan of attack. Their animating spirit was best reflected in the words of the anarchist I. S. Bleikhman, "The street will organize us!"

Impatient insistence that all power be transferred to the soviets foundered on the shoals of moderation: the soviets, dominated by moderate socialists, did not want power; they sided with the government. In addition, key Bolshevik leaders thought the street action precipitous. But passions flared and "the street" tried to reassert its power to change regimes, as it had in February. A rebellious mood was no match for organized force, however. The government brought in loyal troops from the front and street fighting ensued.

The crisis of the July days peaked when on 4 July the government fired on armed demonstrators. Some four hundred people on both sides died. Minister of Justice P. N. Pereverzev launched a double-barreled assault on the Bolsheviks: he sent troops in to smash up the offices of their party newspaper, *Pravda*, arresting everyone present, and he leaked to the progovernment press a packet of documents supposedly proving that Lenin and the other Bolshevik leaders were German agents. This was the boldest and most effective propaganda effort ever mounted by the Provisional Government. Sukhanov noted, "The word 'Bolshevik' had already become synonymous with scoundrel, murderer, Judas, and anybody else whom it was essential to seize, maul, and beat up."[70] The government's allegations persuaded some regiments that had remained neutral to come out into the streets to suppress the demonstra-

tions. Kronstadt sailors returned to their naval bases. Loyal forces retook the Kshesinskaya mansion and the Durnovo villa, arresting everyone they found there. The government decreed that all organizations and leaders of the armed movement against the government, and anyone making appeals or instigating for it, would be arrested and brought to trial as traitors to their nation and the Revolution.[71] Many Bolshevik leaders were arrested; Lenin went into hiding in Finland. He rethought the lessons just learned and came to the realization that the moderate SRs and Mensheviks, who dominated the Soviet, were supporting counterrevolution and that the soviets themselves had become "mere fig leaves of counterrevolution." Instead of advocating "all power to the soviets," Lenin began urging his party to think about seizing power in an armed uprising and then transferring power to the proletariat and peasantry. Trotsky, who was not yet officially a member of the Bolshevik party (he belonged to the small Interdistrict Group that tried to unite Bolsheviks and Mensheviks), remained free for several weeks until he found himself in the same prison in which the tsarist government had locked him up in 1905. Gorky's newspaper carried an editorial: "The counterrevolution is making great strides, not by the day but by the very hour. Searches and arrests—and what notable arrests—the tsar's secret police did not allow itself such insolent conduct, the likes of which the bourgeois youth and Cossack officer have lately undertaken in an effort to 'restore order' in Petrograd."[72]

The repression of this ill-fated rebellion enhanced, at least temporarily, the image of the Provisional Government as firm and decisive. But the victory was Pyrrhic. The government had demonstrated that it could restore order. But it could not restore confidence.

The intense clashes that erupted over the summer created clear-cut divisions among the men seeking leadership positions. The actions of the government, officers, and factory owners greatly exacerbated the already acute social polarization. In the glaring summer light workers, soldiers, and some peasants began to see with clarity the stark contrasts between the parties that represented their mood, aspirations, and interests and those that had irredeemably compromised themselves. Kerensky played a major role in making these distinctions so blatant. The July days coincided with another crisis at the top, the result of which was a reformulation of the government's coalition cabinet. This time Kerensky was officially named prime minister, although he had been the de facto head of the government since Miliukov's ouster. Counting on General Kornilov's reputation for severity and toughness, and on his own ability to use his new commander in chief for his own ends, Kerensky was determined to restore government authority, strengthen the army, and rebuild the officers' morale.

To effect a restoration of order Kerensky knew he would need all the military support he could get, especially as reports started coming in from the countryside about a mounting wave of peasant land seizures, disobedience, and disrespect. Since the summer began, the Provisional Government's procrastination on the land question—its policy of collecting data and studying the issue instead of acting on it—had generated widespread disillusionment. Fealty to the new government meant nothing to the peasants, who had little tolerance for its agents, many of whom had formerly been tsarist agents. It didn't take long for the peasants to learn that the government lacked the force to make its will felt. Obedience gave way to the peasants' own "moral

economy." They began seizing what they believed to be rightfully theirs. Estates were confiscated, property was grabbed. Soldiers—most of whom were peasants in uniform—would seldom attack their brothers for crimes against private property even when they were stationed near a village. Many soldiers deserted the army for home after receiving letters telling them that old scores were being settled and that land was being parceled out among the able-bodied villagers.

Although there were relatively few cases of assaults on landowners, fear of another *Pugachevshchina*, along with the few reported incidents of violence, compelled many nobles to flee to the big cities. In one notable case, ordinary economic grievances, mixed with perverse nationalism, produced gruesome results. In a province on the Volga River, a grain mill, owned by a man with a German name, burned down. Rumors began that the owner himself was the arsonist and that he had set fire to the mill to avenge peasants who complained about his fees. Discretion told him to leave until the peasants' angry mood abated. But, as the historian of this region narrates: "Someone recognized him at the railroad station and a group of soldiers held an impromptu trial and found him guilty. A soldier bashed Teilman in the head with a rifle butt. He was shot and bayoneted. His body was then scooped up on bayonet point and dumped on

The first Provisional Government, headed by Prince Georgy Lvov (fifth from right). Pavel Miliukov is seated to his left, Alexander Kerensky to his right.

the railroad tracks. Threatened by the soldiers, the conductor was forced to drive the engine back and forth over the body. To the horror of those on the train, the soldiers then stuffed cigarettes in the corpse's mouth, set the body on fire and began to dance."[73]

As greater numbers of noblemen abandoned their estates in fear, the countryside became ever more a peasant world disconnected from the urban centers. No wonder photographers seldom ventured outside the cities to capture images of peasant life on bulky glass negatives. The government had increasing difficulty reaching out into the heartland; even getting food became a problem. And things would only get worse.

In late summer even city-based Sukhanov realized how desperate the situation in the countryside had become:

> The peasants, finally losing patience, began settling the agrarian question at first hand— by their own methods. It was impossible not to give them land; it was impossible to torture them any longer by uncertainty. It was impossible to make speeches to them. . . . Estates were divided up and tilled, herds were slaughtered and driven off, country-houses were plundered and destroyed, trees and orchards were chopped down, there was murder and violence. These were no longer "excesses," as they had been in May and June. It was a mass phenomenon—tidal waves heaving and billowing throughout the country.[74]

Meanwhile, Kerensky's promotion of General Kornilov to commander in chief backfired. Workers and soldiers interpreted Kornilov's messages on the need to restore order and discipline as a direct attack on the gains made to date. The reinstitution of the death penalty at the front and the outlawing of strikes were seen by many as nothing less than an assault on the left. A power struggle between the two egoists, Kerensky and Kornilov, each trying to manipulate the other, exploded. Kerensky wanted to preserve his image as a socialist and revolutionary while making Kornilov do the unpleasant work of eliminating the anarchy of freedom as he imposed discipline. But Kornilov, the quintessential "man on the white horse"—the counterrevolutionary military dictator—wanted more than to serve as Kerensky's tool. The real counterrevolutionary position of Kornilov and the resurgent right centered on a belief that only a militarization of industry and transport would save Russia. This demanded an ironfisted central government capable of smashing the soviets and eliminating all elements of workers' control. To Petrograd workers and soldiers, Kornilov's mutinous march on the capital "to restore order" in late August was seen as a repressive attempt to return to the old, prerevolutionary continuities.

The march prompted a great mood swing from the post–July days depression. Workers marshalled their strength to defend the city and, by extension, Kerensky's government; Kornilov's own troops refused to fight. His counterrevolutionary coup fizzled. But when the threat looked the greatest, the Petrograd Soviet formed a special Committee for Struggle against the Counterrevolution. It comprised equal representation (three members each) of Mensheviks, SRs, and Bolsheviks, with the tacit recognition of the Bolsheviks' growing stature among the workers. In fact, the Bolsheviks played a telling role in the committee, as Sukhanov noted:

> The committee, making preparation for defense, had to mobilize the worker-soldier masses. But the masses, however much they were organized, were organized by the Bolsheviks. They followed the Bolsheviks. At that time, theirs was the only organization that was large, held together by an elementary discipline, and linked with the democratic lowest levels of the capital. Without it the committee was impotent. Without the Bolsheviks, it could only have passed time issuing appeals and having men who had already lost their authority make speeches. With the Bolsheviks, the committee had at its disposal the full power of the organized workers and soldiers.[75]

After Kornilov's attempted coup failed, workers remained armed. Those who had formed neighborhood or factory militias to defend the Revolution were soon being called Red Guards. The Kornilov march, following on the heels of July, did more than any other single event to increase the radicalization of the workers and widen the gulf between the people and the government, discrediting everyone associated with the latter in the eyes of the former.

EXTREMISM IN DEFENSE OF LIBERTY

This radicalization greatly benefited the Bolsheviks; as impatience grew, so did their popularity. But the Bolsheviks were not alone. Adopting an almost British air of understatement, John Reed observed in his famous *Ten Days That Shook the World,* "To the average reader the multiplicity of Russian organizations—political groups, committees . . . will prove extremely confusing."[76] Born out of traditions very different from those in the West and subject to frequent schisms that produced a plethora of parties, factions, and groupings, the Russian political scene struck many Westerners as virtually incomprehensible. Historical perspective, however, and a breakdown of the different entities' positions on key issues that determined political popularity, such as the war, help make it more understandable. As impatience with those continuing the war grew during the summer, only the parties categorically against it, all leftist, benefited from the rising radical tide. Anarchists, Left Socialist Revolutionaries, and Menshevik-Internationalists were identified in the popular mind with an untainted commitment to change. The Menshevik-Internationalists, like the Bolsheviks, adhered to the Zimmerwald principles, which held that any use of military force for national purposes was unacceptable and that an immediate end to the imperialist war was imperative. To varying degrees all of these parties were seen as free from compromising ties either with the old regime, the Provisional Government, or the superordination of the ruling classes. Unlike the moderate socialist parties—the Mensheviks and Socialist Revolutionaries, who had dominated the soviets up to this point and had entered into a coalition with the Provisional Government—the above-named leftist parties could not be charged with having been

The bearded Prince P. A. Kropotkin
■ (1842–1921), a prominent Anarchist.

co-opted by the class enemy, the bourgeoisie. Neither were they subject to charges of betraying the Revolution by supporting repression in factories or bloody offenses at the front.

All of these leftist parties, however, remained less than major actors on the political stage. The Anarchists suffered from internal divisions, implacable opposition to any kind of central authority, including their own party leaders, and anathematization as the most extreme of the extremist groups. The Anarchists believed in direct action and eschewed hierarchical structures. They held that effective emancipation could be realized only if the workers themselves—not grouped as a party or under anyone's leadership—acting on the basis of their own class organizations (unions, factory committees, cooperatives, local soviets), made a revolution. They stressed that even anarchists could not guide a revolution from the outside; it had to be a mass movement, at best helped by anarchists, otherwise the results would be simply illusory. Free will was beautiful and inspirational, but a little too abstract for many in 1917.

The Left Socialist Revolutionaries' emergence out of the largest, but certainly not the strongest, party presented special difficulties. Carving out a distinctive identity took time. In Petrograd, for instance, Left SRs split from the quickly disintegrating Socialist Revolutionary party. They wrested control of the party organization from more moderate Socialist Revolutionaries and renamed it. Only in September did the Left SRs get their own consistently published newspaper. A reputation as a group led by wholly utopian, wild-eyed people did not help.

The Menshevik-Internationalists had a different order of problems. This small offshoot of the party that headed the Soviet from its inception was committed to a scrupulously precise revolutionary democracy. But its very intellectualism, its exactness, and its predominantly Jewish leadership, epitomized by its greatly respected leader Martov, precluded broad popularity. Nor was its highly principled approach suited to an emotionally charged epoch. "Our Marxist theories," one activist observed, "were incomprehensible and irritating to the masses, which had just barely tasted the blessing of free political development."[77] The Menshevik-Internationalists held positions closely corresponding to the aspirations of the increasingly politicized Petrograd masses, yet they lacked the popular appeal and aggressive leadership necessary to turn their concepts into political power.

Although they played in a minor key, these leftist parties—especially the Anarchists and Left SRs—harmonized with the Bolsheviks' major key, which was resounding loud and clear in Petrograd and elsewhere.

At the end of the summer new elections to the municipal Duma (city self-government) were held in Petrograd and Moscow. Both capitals recorded major gains for the Bolsheviks. Early in September,

Railroad workers, key activists ■ in the Revolution, declare a nationwide strike on 23 September.

representatives to the Petrograd Soviet who had been elected in the spring were replaced by new men who reflected the increasingly militant mood of workers and soldiers, and the Bolsheviks obtained a majority for the first time. In the All-Russian Executive Committee (of Workers', Soldiers', and Peasants' Soviets), the Menshevik-Internationalist Martov proposed the creation of an all-socialist ministry responsible to a democratic parliament. Although this proposal was rejected, it was a sign of the radical times and of the complete alienation from the Kerensky government. On 16 October, when Petrograd's most aggressive revolutionary elements formed a Military Revolutionary Committee—the group that would be directly responsible for the physical overthrow of Kerensky's last Provisional Government—a Bolshevik majority shared leadership with Left SRs (forty-eight Bolsheviks, fourteen Left SRs, and four Anarchists comprised the committee).[78] This ostensibly nonparty, insurrectionary organ was headed by Left SR Pavel Lazimir and Bolsheviks Antonov-Ovseenko and Trotsky.

Over the course of 1917 the Bolsheviks became the most popular and powerful radical party in the capitals. Their class-based interpretation of the Revolution made sense to workers, increasingly so in the summer, when the old order, favoring the propertied classes and prerevolutionary values, threatened to reassert itself at the workers' expense. The Bolsheviks—or more specifically their program for a simple resolution of the land question—also gained an enthusiastic following among the peasants. In Russia's vast countryside, as elsewhere, the ground swell of support for this party derived from its clear articulation of popular aspirations.

Bolshevik slogans, brilliant in their direct, simple, radical formulation—"Peace, Bread, Land"; "All Power to the Soviets!"—captured the attention of the alienated masses. Significantly, it was the masses themselves, particularly the working classes crowded into Russia's cities, who shaped party policy as much as they were shaped by it. Their dreams and fears found a voice in these terribly effective slogans, which can be seen in so many photographs. The Bolsheviks' genius for sloganeering was a matter of articulation, not manipulation. The radicalized masses gave them the message, the party wordsmith gave them a medium.

From March on, the contrast between the Provisional Government's continuing commitment to the war and the Bolsheviks' unrelenting opposition to it grew sharper and sharper. The impossible goal of simultaneously pursuing war to victory and resolving all the social problems brought to the surface by the collapse of the old order eventually destroyed the Provisional Government. The longer the war continued, the more popular the Bolsheviks became. Mounting defeats turned people away from the new establishment. When the Baltic Sea port of Riga fell to the Germans in late August, the event boldly dramatized the government's impotence. Yet even when Kerensky's own cabinet members advised him, in the most direct way possible, to start peace negotiations, he proved incapable of abandoning the war to save his government. Just before the October Revolution, General A. I. Verkhovsky, then minister of war, reported:

> The situation at the front is a disaster. . . .
> There is no way out. No palliative measures exist for restoring the army's fighting powers that can overcome the destructive influence of the peace propaganda. We are at an impasse. The only possible way to combat the pernicious influence of the Bolsheviks is to pull the rug out from under them by immediately proposing to make peace ourselves. News of peace talks . . . will lay the basis for restoring the army to health. By relying on the units that remain most intact we could find it possible to forcibly suppress anarchy in the country.[79]

An angry Kerensky fired Verkhovsky for this insight.

The Bolsheviks clearly stood for a particular class point of view. They did not try to be all things to all people; they did not pretend to stand above partisan interests for the greater good of some abstract nation-state. The Bolsheviks openly identified themselves with the insurgents against the incumbents. As spokesmen for the exploited they attacked the exploiters. Instead of seeking a way to mend the country's social fabric, they were busy trying to harness the energy that would be released by tearing it apart.

Workers became Bolsheviks because the Bolshevik party represented change, not continuity. The working-class identity found resonance in the Bolsheviks' goals, slogans, and fierce oppositional approach. As experience taught workers intolerance for the Provisional Government's foot-dragging on basic social reforms, as well as for its stubborn continuation of the war, the Bolsheviks' uncompromising militancy and class analysis of the situation grew more attractive.

Moreover, the party's open enrollment policy, instituted in 1917, swelled its ranks dramatically and lent it a mass character. As more and more working-class people became radicalized, they sought affiliation with a party. In a very complicated, often subtle (but often unsubtle too) process, workers identified their interests with those of the Bolshevik party. The party had an unusual responsiveness to people's emotions. If the axiom that all politics are local is true, then the Bolsheviks' relatively decentralized structure and method of operation gave it a great deal of power. The party's mass, democratic character, combined with its tolerance for divergent points of view, made its meetings, at all levels, lively. Differing opinions, theoretical and tactical, flew back and forth. Dissident or minority voices could be heard without censure. Those fighting for heretical views could, and did, on occasion, reverse the set course. Minds could be changed— or not changed—without fear of expulsion from the party. It was democratization, not dictatorship, that made the Bolsheviks so powerful and popular in 1917.

This relatively tolerant, democratic atmosphere gave the Bolsheviks' remarkably talented leaders free rein to develop ideas, tactics, and strategies. The party possessed a stable of inspiring speakers, including Zinoviev, Bukharin, Kollantai, and, of course, Lenin, but none was more powerful than the newcomer Trotsky. Lenin may not have been the best speaker among them, but he was the embodiment of that very rare phenomenon, the charismatic leader. With his acute insight, soaring intellect, and relentless, logical presentation of ideas, he inspired fervent devotion among the small inner circle of Bolshevik leaders. In larger gatherings, he produced a virtual magnetic field, captivating listeners and energizing them with his revolutionary faith and incisive analysis.

Even rarer than his abilities as a charismatic leader was his place as a "hero in history." From his arrival at the Finland Station in April, when he reversed party policy, setting it in direct opposition to the Provisional Government, until late summer, when he hammered away at the party's Central Committee for a commitment to an armed uprising, he used his political genius to turn history's course. From his hiding place in Finland, Lenin barraged the Central Committee, the political brain of the party, with critiques and sharply worded exhortations. He argued, scolded, shamed, and even tendered his resignation to convince his fellow party leaders to take up his initiative and prepare for an armed overthrow of the Provisional Government. In September, for instance, when some wanted to wait and see what a nationwide congress of representatives from the various soviets would say, he furiously argued:

> To wait for the Congress of Soviets is idiocy, for the congress will give nothing and can give nothing. . . . We have thousands of armed workers and soldiers in Petrograd who at once could seize the Winter Palace, the General Staff building, the telephone exchange, and the large printing presses. If we were to attack at once, suddenly, from three points—Petrograd, Moscow, and the Baltic fleet, the chances are a hundred to one that we would succeed with lesser sacrifices than those suffered on 3–5 July. . . .

> I am compelled to tender my resignation from the Central Committee, which I hereby do, reserving for myself the freedom to campaign among the party rank and file and at the party congress. For it is my profound conviction that if we "wait" for the Congress of Soviets and let the present moment pass, we will ruin the revolution.[80]

The Central Committee might not have always listened to Lenin, but it certainly would not accept his resignation. Much depended on the freewheeling, democratic nature of the party. In late September, leaders who had their fingers on the pulse of the Petrograd masses resisted Lenin's appeals for an immediate insurrection, calling them ill-timed. Only in late October, when a syzygy of Lenin's arguments, the Central Committee's acceptance, the Military Revolutionary Committee's careful preparations (under the leadership of Trotsky, Antonov-Ovseenko et al.), and the popular mood occurred, did the Bolsheviks come to power.

Rumors of a Bolshevik coup d'état swirled through the capital. On 18 October Gorky warned: "Rumors are more and more persistently being spread that 'some action by the Bolsheviks' will take place on October 20; in other words, the disgusting scenes of July 3–5 may be repeated. . . . All the dark instincts of the crowd irritated by the disintegration of life and by the lies and filth of politics will flare up and fume, poisoning us with anger, hate, and revenge; people will kill one another, unable to suppress their own animal stupidity."[81]

Left SRs, in general, and those in the Military Revolutionary Committee, in particular, were inclined not to seize power, but to force a transfer of all authority from the discredited Kerensky government to a revolutionary one, a coalition of the left socialists who would be gathering for the Second All-Russian Congress of Soviets. Boris Kamkov voiced their sentiments:

> Let us not play hide and seek with each other. Is there anybody who would trust this government? . . . It does not have the support of the revolutionary army, or the proletariat, and coming out against it is not the rabble [as Kerensky claimed] but precisely the most politically conscious elements of revolutionary democracy. If we are seriously interested in eliminating the soil in which the horrors of civil war are maturing, we must openly declare that the only way out of the present predicament is through the creation of a homogeneous, revolutionary, democratic government. . . .[82]

Short of seizing power, the Left SRs were well-disposed toward taking all necessary measures to protect against counterrevolution and to undercut the Kerensky government.

The Military Revolutionary Committee actually brought about the Revolution. Led by Trotsky, from 20–24 October it slyly undercut support for the Provisional Government. Subversion rather than frontal assault characterized its method of operation. Individual members of the Military Revolutionary Committee forged vital links with various troop garrisons. Oddly, Kerensky's provocative actions helped Trotsky and the Bolsheviks win over the troops and accelerated the Revolution's momentum. Soldiers and sailors stationed in the capital grew increasingly restive in mid-October when Kerensky announced plans to send the majority of them to the front. The Provisional Government thought it had made a crafty dual-purpose decision: it would bolster the front against the Germans, who seemed now to threaten the capital itself, and it would simultaneously rid Petrograd of dangerous troops inclined toward the extreme revolutionary posture of the Bolsheviks, Left SRs, and Mensheviks. Instead, the government solidified the amorphous support for the Bolsheviks and provided a fiery cause against which to organize an armed mass revolt. Unit after unit voted for a declaration of no confidence in the government and called for a transfer of "all power to the soviets." Fear of counterrevolutionary onslaughts à la Kornilov, as well as meaningless deaths under the Provisional Government's inept command, fueled the revolutionary mood. Men in the Military Revolutionary Committee stood firm against transfers to the front and created a "garrison conference" for staff in touch with the troops to keep increasingly "Red Petrograd" from being bled white.

Sukhanov saw all this as marking a turning point. "On October 21st the Petrograd garrison conclusively acknowledged the Soviet as sole power and the Military Revolutionary Committee as the immediate organ of authority."[83] Taking over the role of the organization that authorized any orders, the committee powerfully subverted the government. Soldiers loyal to the revolutionary committee

The Peter and Paul Fortress cannon ■ firing its noon signal.
BOTTOM
Red Guards and soldiers on ■ patrol in Petrograd during the October Revolution.

turned over most of the capital's arsenals to radicals, who, in turn, opened storehouses of firearms to Red Guard sympathizers. Petrograd became a very well armed city, with few guns in the hands of people loyal to the Kerensky government. The government summoned all the troops it could. They brought an all-female unit, the Women's Shock Battalion of Death—more famous for its name than its combat effectiveness—as well as some cadets from a military school to guard the Winter Palace. The stacks of cordwood placed around it in preparation for another long, cold winter protected the great building better than these poor excuses for soldiers.

Troops at key installations put themselves at the revolutionaries' disposal. For instance, the symbolically and militarily significant Peter and Paul

Fortress, whose massive silhouette loomed over the Winter Palace, went over to the Military Revolutionary Committee after hours of speechmaking. Fortress machine guns were capable of sweeping the range of a key bridge over the Neva. The fortress had but a single cannon, the one that daily signaled the noon hour, but there were artillery guns inside. More than a military or political presence, the fortress played an important psychological role. Trotsky appeared not so much to speak, as one observer put it, but to offer "an inspirational song."[84] By open vote the troops literally turned their backs on Kerensky's government. They put at least one hundred thousand rifles in the Bolsheviks' hands[85] and offered them the fortress as an alternative headquarters if counterrevolution forced them from the Smolny (formerly a school for daughters of the nobility located on the outskirts of the capital, where the Petrograd Soviet and the Central Executive Committee had moved in July).

Just as he had helped accelerate the garrisons' change of allegiance by ordering them to the front, Kerensky precipitated the Bolsheviks' decisive push to seize power by once again ordering the closing of their press. "Incitement to insurrection" was the grounds cited. Remembering actions in July, protective steps were taken. The bridges over the Neva were guarded to keep traffic flowing between various parts of the city. The Military Revolutionary Committee paid careful attention to the most strategic points, but somehow some cadets from a military school who had been guarding one bridge for the government managed to raise it. This moment has been immortalized by the great filmmaker Eisenstein in *October* or *Ten Days That Shook the World*; the scene depicts a wagon and a dead horse sliding over the edge of the slowly rising bridge ramp before revolutionary troops could close it. In another step to prevent a repetition of July, armed bands moved to protect the Smolny. Sukhanov explained:

> Smolny now had a quite impregnable look. Detachments of sailors, soldiers, and armed workers were posted around and inside the enormous building. There were quite a few machine guns in the square, besides the can-

non. Lorries, on which were crowded people with rifles and other weapons, were making a deafening racket. Now it was no longer possible to arrest the Military Revolutionary Committee, or bring up a detachment of 500 men to *occupy* this nest of insurgents. Now Smolny could only be *besieged and stormed*. This would no longer have been a simple "measure" of a powerful Government, but an act of civil war.[86]

The fortification of the Smolny lacked anything approaching military precision. Like much that occurred in October, it drew its breath from the vola-

Soldiers guarding the entrance ■ to the Smolny, headquarters of the Military Revolutionary Committee.

BOTTOM

Sentries vigilantly checking ■ documents at the Smolny gates.

tile air of improvisation. John Reed, an American correspondent and radical sympathizer on the scene, observed:

> I spent a great deal of time at Smolny. It was no longer easy to get in. Double rows of sentries guarded the outer gates, and once inside the front door there was a long line of people waiting to be let in. . . . Passes were given out and the pass system was changed every few hours; for spies continually sneaked through. . . . One day as I came up to the outer gate I saw Trotsky and his wife just ahead of me. They were halted by a soldier. Trotsky searched through his pockets, but could find no pass. "Never mind," he said finally, "You know me. My name is Trotsky." "You haven't got a pass," answered the soldier stubbornly. "You cannot go in. Names don't mean anything to me." "But I am the president of the Petrograd Soviet." "Well," replied the soldier, "if you're as important a fellow as that you must at least have one little paper." Trotsky was very patient. "Let me see the Commandant," he said. The soldier hesitated, grumbled about not wanting to disturb the Commandant for every devil that came along. He beckoned finally to the soldier in command of the guard. Trotsky explained matters to him. "My name is Trotsky," he repeated. "Trotsky?" The other soldier scratched his head. "I've heard the name somewhere," he said at length. "I guess it's all right. You can go on in, comrade."[87]

The Smolny, where the Military Revolutionary Committee, the Central Committee of the Bolshevik party, the Petrograd Soviet, its Executive Committee, and other bodies met, was the nerve center of the Revolution. Orders to execute the overthrow of the Provisional Government emanated from here the night of 24–25 October. The Military Revolutionary Committee, which had been acting to defend the Revolution, went on the offensive that night. Lenin made the difference, Lenin forced the issue. With a warrant for his arrest still outstanding, he disguised himself and made his way from an apartment hideout across Petrograd by trolley and by foot to the Smolny. As one American historian hostile to the Bolsheviks was to admit, Lenin's arrival "electrified the entire soviet headquarters. There is reason to believe that Lenin by direct command or perhaps by his mere presence, had a decisive effect in changing the orientation of his lieutenants from the defensive to the offensive."[88] Very aggressive new tactics became the order of the day.

Bolsheviks dispatched by the Military Revolutionary Committee secured the telegraph exchange and the telephone switchboards, restoring service to the Smolny and cutting off the Winter Palace; they

The telephone exchange, after it was taken by the Military Revolutionary Committee.

took over electrical stations, removing power from most government offices. Red Guards surrounded the Winter Palace, secured bridges and train stations, and seized the government car pool. Sailors took over the State Bank. Revolutionary sailors from the Baltic fleet, which was bottled up in Helsinki, responded to the booming voice and inspirational leadership of the Bolshevik P. E. Dybenko, chairman of their soviet, when he summoned them to aid the armed uprising. The committee signaled radical sailors on the cruiser *Aurora*, just out of dry dock, to move up the Neva. It was to bring its guns to bear on a key bridge and to stand ready to shell the Winter Palace. The ship also served as a floating radio station, transmitting revolutionary messages to the fleet and the front.

The cruiser *Aurora*, whose guns ■ frighten the Provisional Government into final surrender.

BOTTOM

Crowds flock to the Winter Palace after ■ the Provisional Government's downfall.

The early morning of 25 October found Kerensky and his cabinet effectively isolated in the Winter Palace; virtually no one in Petrograd came to their aid. Kerensky decided to leave the capital in search of dependable army or Cossack units capable of defending the government and countering the revolutionary forces. His aides managed to secure a two-car caravan to whisk the prime minister out of the hostile city; one car, belonging to a secretary at the American embassy, flew a protective American flag, while the other, a Russian-owned Pierce-Arrow, carried Kerensky toward the front.

Meanwhile, most of the Provisional Government's cabinet continued meeting in the Winter Palace. Under the command of Antonov-Ovseenko,

soldiers, Red Guards, and sailors surrounded and isolated the massive structure. Three thousand sailors from the nearby Kronstadt naval base arrived on a series of ships and came ashore to help secure the heart of Petrograd. Some occupied the neighboring admiralty building, others manned armored cars and stood picket duty on Palace Square. All day long delays frustrated those clamoring for an immediate assault on this last citadel of the old regime. Slowly but surely, the few cadets and handful of Cossacks protecting the palace melted away. As night fell, Antonov-Ovseenko dispatched an ultimatum to whom he thought was Kerensky and his cabinet, ordering them to surrender in twenty minutes or else the Military Revolutionary Committee would shell the palace from the Peter and Paul Fortress, the *Aurora*, and other ships. The minutes flew by. After overcoming a series of obstacles in an attempt to find and rig up a red signal lantern at the fortress, the committee finally managed to signal the *Aurora* to make good on their threat. The great ship's bow gun fired one enormously loud round of blanks that thundered and reverberated throughout the city. Some of the remaining government troops fled, including most of the women's battalion. After a pause to allow for quick exits from the palace, artillerymen at the fortress began shooting at the building. A few shells blasted windows on the floor above the cabinet's meeting place. This convinced the last ministers of the last Provisional Government that discretion was the better part of valor.

There was no dramatic storming of the Winter Palace. In the small hours of the morning Antonov-Ovseenko calculated that the *Aurora*, the artillery shells, and the massive number of revolutionary troops surrounding the palace had frightened off all but the last guardians of the old order. He led his forces into the palace. The only resistance they encountered was the building's own confusing maze of corridors and almost one thousand rooms, many of which were littered with evidence of the soldiers who had been encamped there for months. Antonov-Ovseenko, surprised not to find Kerensky among the remaining ministers, arrested them and marched them off to damp cells in the Peter and Paul Fortress.

Their arrest and incarceration provided proof of the declaration that Lenin had penned and the Military Revolutionary Committee had issued the previous morning, coincidentally at about the same time Kerensky was fleeing the capital.

To the Citizens of Russia.

The Provisional Government has been overthrown. State power has passed into the hands of the organ of the Petrograd Soviet of Workers' and Soldiers' Deputies, the Military Revolutionary Committee, which stands at the head of the Petrograd proletariat and garrison.

The cause for which the people have struggled—the immediate proposal of a democratic peace, the elimination of the landlord estates, workers' control over production, the creation of a soviet government—the triumph of this cause has been assured.

Long live the workers', soldiers', and peasants' revolution![89]

A new order quickly asserted itself. In the Winter Palace, John Reed witnessed its spontaneous implementation: "One man went strutting around with a bronze clock perched on his shoulder; another found a plume of ostrich feathers which he stuck in his hat. The looting was just beginning when somebody cried, 'Comrades! Don't touch anything! Don't take anything! This is the property of the people!' . . . 'Clear the palace!' bawled a Red Guard, sticking his head through an inner door. 'Come, comrades, let's show that we're not thieves and bandits.'"[90]

Late in the evening of 25 October the new order was confirmed in a more substantive way by the Second All-Russian Congress of Soviets at the Smolny. By proportional representation the Bolsheviks claimed fourteen seats in the Presidium and the Left SRs seven. The Mensheviks were allotted three, the Menshevik-Internationalists one. Almost immediately, the main body of Mensheviks and Right SRs walked out to protest the Bolsheviks' precipitous actions. When Menshevik-Internationalist leader Martov rose to propose the formation of "an all-democratic government" of all the socialist parties

Announcement of the fall of the Provisional Government.

as a way of precluding a conspiratorial seizure of power from provoking a counterrevolution and civil war, he was met by an animated reaction from Trotsky: "A rising of the masses of the people requires no justification. What has happened is an insurrection, and not a conspiracy. We harnessed the revolutionary energy of the Petersburg workers and soldiers. . . . now we are told: Renounce your victory, make concessions, compromises. . . . No, here no compromise is possible. To those who have left and to those who tell us to do this we must say: You are miserable bankrupts, your role is played out: go to where you ought to go—into the dustbin of history!"[91]

Several hours later the Menshevik-Internationalists, too, stomped out of the hall. At 5:00 A.M. the Congress of Soviets adopted Lenin's manifesto, "To All Workers, Soldiers, and Peasants." It authorized the transfer of political authority into the hands of the congress and local soviets throughout the land. It promised bread, land, peace, and self-

Election posters for the
Constituent Assembly.

determination for all nationalities. It called on soldiers in the trenches to be steadfast in their resistance to Kerensky's counterrevolutionary actions. It called on railwaymen to stop all echelons sent by Kerensky against Petrograd. This document legitimized Soviet power; it also marked the Bolsheviks' official conquest of power in Petrograd.

EXPERIENCING REVOLUTION

In the great school of revolution that was 1917, the people learned enormously. Much of its success depended on the growing class consciousness of the working masses, much on a consciousness of the failings of the Provisional Government. Much also depended on spontaneity and improvisation. The

Bolsheviks learned how much procrastination and bureaucratic procedure had alienated the masses. They quickly issued decrees and proclamations addressing fundamental issues. They called for an immediate peace without annexations and without indemnities. They proclaimed an end to secret diplomacy and moved to publish all secret treaties. Elections to a Constituent Assembly were announced for 12 November under rules and election slates worked out months before. They abolished private ownership of land. They issued rules for the confiscation and redistribution of all land. They abolished capital punishment—which had been restored by Kerensky during the summer—at the front. They transferred all authority in the provinces to local soviets. Bolshevik leaders also improvised; Trotsky and Lenin thought up a name for their new kind of government: Council of People's Commissars. They thought the word *commissar* splendid because, as Lenin put it, "it stinks of revolution."

Petrograd was the capital, but it wasn't the country. Elsewhere the battle for Soviet power took different turns. In Moscow street fighting replaced the uneasy civil calm that had reigned since late summer. A Military Revolutionary Committee, formed on 25 October, clashed with a Committee of Public Safety, a group of supporters of the Provisional Government who opposed Soviet power. Barricades appeared on some of the same streets where they had stood in 1905; long-range guns on Sparrow Hills (now the site of Moscow University) barraged the city. Red Guards, soldiers, and armed citizens shot at each other across Red Square. Moscow workers threw themselves into the fight, not as much to seize power as to fight against counter-revolution. However militant Moscow's working classes were, they were ill-prepared and badly organized for this task. Unlike their Petrograd brothers, they had no great storehouse of weapons at their disposal. All of this made for a prolonged battle. The two sides contested possession of the Kremlin; it changed hands several times. Rumors circulated that whoever lost control of this citadel planned to blow it up. This never happened, but insurgents lobbed artillery shells against the imposing fortress. Soviet forces retook the Kremlin on 2 November, capping a military victory. In other cities, local political and social personalities dictated the course of their struggles for power.

The prolonged Moscow contest had important consequences for the infant Soviet regime. While the outcome still hung in the balance, the powerful socialist but non-Bolshevik executive committee of the railroad union threatened a rail strike—an action that would have cut Moscow off from Petrograd—if the new Soviet government was not reconstituted to include representatives of other socialist parties. A few weeks later, after lengthy negotiations and heated internal debates, the Left SRs entered a new coalition government. Most prominent among them was I. N. Steinberg, who became the commissar of justice. This change from a one-party system helped the Bolsheviks gain support in the villages, where the Left SR solution to the land issue, adopted virtually in toto by the Bolsheviks, enjoyed immense popularity.

To sustain the Revolution nationally, the new Soviet government, headed by Lenin, had to count on a shared sense of revolutionary accomplishment, of identification with the Revolution. Each village, each provincial town, each city, each army regiment experienced the Revolution in its own way, as did every individual. Boris Pasternak captured this in his novel *Dr. Zhivago*:

> The revolution broke out willy-nilly, like a sigh suppressed too long. Everyone was revived, reborn, changed, transformed. You might say that everyone has been through two revolutions—his own personal revolution as well as the general one. It seems to me that socialism is the sea, and all these separate streams, these private individual revolutions are flowing into it—the sea of life, the sea of spontaneity. I said life, but I mean life as you see it in a great picture, transformed by genius, creatively enriched. Only now people have decided to experience it not in books and pictures but in themselves, not as an abstraction but in practice.[92]

Left SR Isaak Steinberg, ■ Commissar of Justice.

The Bolsheviks themselves had barely survived badly managed acts of suppression. They were not about to give up the power they had fought so hard for by failing to hobble their enemies. Knowing well how much power a counterrevolution could give to an insurgent movement, the new Bolshevik regime was determined to suppress Kerensky and other opponents. In one key battle a red workers' militia and a contingent of Baltic fleet sailors defeated a Kerensky-inspired Cossack force, led by General Krasnov, at Pulkovo Heights on the outskirts of Petrograd. The new government's leaders returned the favor of censorship that had been imposed on them by the Provisional Government; they quickly closed down newspapers trying to incite armed opposition. This prohibition provoked Gorky's ire: "Lenin, Trotsky, and their companions have already become poisoned with the filthy venom of power, and this is evidenced by their shameful attitude towards freedom of speech, the individual and the sum total of those rights for the triumph of which democracy struggled." In a subsequent, more philosophical passage he commented: "And I am especially suspicious, especially distrustful, of a Russian when he gets power into his hands. Not long ago a slave, he has become the most unbridled despot as soon as he has the chance to become his neighbor's master."[93]

The sweeping liberation of the Revolution impelled some toward disorderly conduct. Crowds helped themselves to the bounty of imperial wine cellars. Some fire trucks had to be dispatched to pump out vast storehouses of liquor to prevent the spread of that very Russian disease, drunkenness. Kerensky's former private secretary recalled walking through Petrograd: "I came on a crowd of soldiers plundering a wineshop. Already brutally drunk, they yelled: 'Long life to the Bolsheviki and death to the capitalistic government!' . . . Huge crowds of soldiers, sailors and workmen plundered the cellars of the Winter Palace. Broken bottles littered the square, cries, shrieks, groans, obscenities, filled the clean morning. . . . The cellars swam in wine from broken casks and bottles and many men were actually drowned in the flood of it."[94]

Such seemingly trivial issues threatened public order and thus endangered the fledgling regime. Lenin believed, "The bourgeoisie is having recourse to the vilest crimes, bribing society's lowest elements and supplying liquor to these outcasts, to provoke pogroms." Even more worrisome were strikes by white-collar government employees, which the new authorities saw as acts of sabotage. "Bank clerks, etc. are sabotaging and organizing strikes in order to block the government's effort to reconstruct the state on a socialist basis."[95] In early December the Soviet government established an "All-Russian Extraordinary Commission for the Suppression of Counterrevolution and Sabotage"— known by its acronym, the Cheka.

The new Soviet government, brilliantly led by Lenin, knew that it had to act deliberately and decisively. To protect the Revolution it had to focus on fundamental questions of power. As John Reed observed in his remarkable chronicle: "The only reason for Bolshevik success lay in their accomplishing the vast and simple desires of the most profound strata of the people, calling them to the work of tearing down and destroying the old, and afterward, in the smoke of falling ruins, cooperating with them to erect the framework of the new. . . ."[96]

To retain power the Bolsheviks would need to improvise and to learn quickly. The sharp social division that brought them to power would soon draw so taut that it would split the country in a civil war. It would take years for the Bolsheviks, the most realistic and flexible of the parties in 1917, to bring their countrymen "peace, bread, and land." The Revolution changed many things; it may not have changed the Russian people, but it did redirect their destiny.

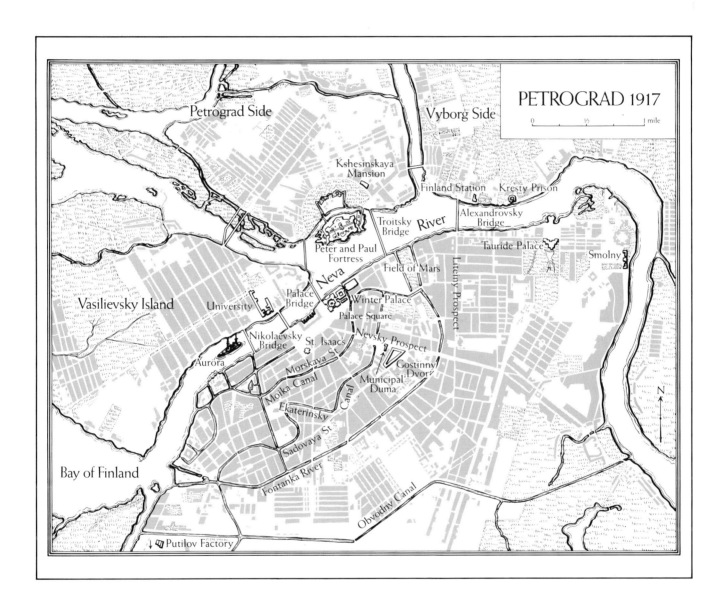

PETROGRAD 1917

0   ½   1 mile

Petrograd Side

Vyborg Side

Kshesinskaya
Mansion

Finland Station   Kresty Prison

Alexandrovsky
Bridge

Troitsky
Bridge

River

Tauride Palace

Smolny

Peter and Paul
Fortress

Neva

Field of Mars

Liteiny Prospect

Vasilievsky Island

University

Palace
Bridge

Winter Palace

Palace Square

Nikolaevsky
Bridge

St. Isaac's

Nevsky Prospect

Aurora

Morskaya St.

Gostinny
Dvor

Moika Canal

Municipal
Duma

Canal

Ekaterinsky

Sadovaya St.

Bay of Finland

Fontanka River

Obvodny Canal

↓ 🏭 Putilov Factory

N

NOTES

1. *Osvobozhdenie*, no. 63 (1904): 230.

2. M. P. Pogodin, as quoted in N. P. Barsukov, *Zhizn' i trudy M. P. Pogodina*, vol. 16 (St. Petersburg, 1902), p. 591.

3. V. O. Klyuchevsky, *Sochineniya v vos'mi tomakh*, 8 vols. (Moscow, 1956–59), vol. 1, p. 313.

4. Paul Avrich, *Russian Rebels, 1600–1880* (New York: Schocken Books, 1972), p. 212.

5. Nicholas I in V. V. Golubtsov, ed., "Imperator Nikolai Pavlovich v ego rechi k deputatam Sanktpeterburgskogo dvoryanstva 21 marta 1848 g.," *Russkaya starina* 40 (September 1883): 595.

6. Basil Dmytryshyn, ed., *Imperial Russia: A Source Book, 1700–1917* (New York: Holt, Rinehart & Winston, 1967), p. 241.

7. *KPSS v rezolyutsiyakh i resheniyakh* (Moscow, 1953), vol. 1, p. 12.

8. Semyon Kanatchikov, *Iz istorii moego bytiya* (Moscow-Leningrad, 1929), pp. 68–69, 10.

9. V. I. Gurko, *Features and Figures of the Past*, The Hoover Library on War, Revolution, and Peace Publication no. 14 (Stanford, California: Stanford University Press, 1939), p. 319.

10. William Chamberlin, *The Russian Revolution, 1917–1921*, 2 vols. (Princeton, New Jersey: Princeton University Press, 1987), vol. 1, p. 41.

11. S. Iu. Witte, *Vospominaniya: Tsarstvovanie Nikolaya II*, 2 vols. (Berlin, 1922), vol. 1, p. 239.

12. L. N. Pushkarev et al., eds., *Nachalo pervoi russkoi revolyutsii, yanvar'-mart, 1905 goda* (Moscow, 1955), pp. 28–31.

13. S. E. Kryzhanovsky, *Vospominaniya* (Berlin, n.d.), pp. 115, 117.

14. Roberta Thompson Manning, *The Crisis of the Old Order in Russia: Gentry and Government* (Princeton, New Jersey: Princeton University Press, 1982), p. 331.

15. Andrew M. Verner, "Nicholas II and the Role of the Autocrat during the First Russian Revolution, 1904–1907" (Ph.D. diss., Columbia University, 1986), p. 105.

16. P. E. Shchegolev, ed., *Padanie tsarskogo rezhima* (Berlin, 1924–27), vol. 5, pp. 372–73.

17. Heinz-Dietrich Löwe, *Antisemitismus und reaktionäre Utopie: russischer Konservatismus im Kampf gegen den Wandel von Staat und Gesellschaft, 1890–1917* (Hamburg, West Germany: Hoffmann und Campe Verlag, 1978), pp. 99, 100.

18. *Padanie*, vol. 4, p. 9.

19. As quoted in Graf Vladimir N. Kokovtsov, *Iz moego proshlogo: Vospominaniya, 1903–1919* (Paris: 1933), vol. 2, p. 42.

20. Sir Bernard Pares, *The Fall of the Russian Monarchy* (London: 1939), p. 397.

21. Paul Miliukov, *Political Memoirs, 1905–1917*, ed. Arthur Mendel (Ann Arbor, Michigan: University of Michigan Press, 1967), p. 305.

22. V. A. Lavrin, *Bolshevistskaya partiya v nachale pervoi mirovoi imperialisticheskoi voiny* (Moscow, 1972), pp. 191, 222.

23. Konstantin Paustovsky, *A Story of Life* (New York: Pantheon, 1982), p. 266.

24. V. V. Shul'gin, *Dni* (Belgrade, Yugoslavia: Rad, n.d.), p. 76.

25. A. A. Brusilov, *Moi vospominaniya* (Moscow-Leningrad, 1929), p. 138.

26. Dmitrii I. Abrikossow, *Revelations of a Russian Diplomat* (Seattle: University of Washington Press, 1964), p. 238.

27. Nicholas II, *Letters of the Tsar to the Tsaritsa, 1914–1917*, trans. A. Hynes from the official edition of the Romanov correspondence (Stanford, California: Hoover Institution Press, 1973), p. 71.

28. Michael T. Florinsky, *The End of the Russian Empire* (New York: Colliers, 1971), p. 67.

29. K. Nabokov, *Ordeal of a Diplomat* (London: Duckworth and Co., 1921), p. 53.

30. "Philip Jordan's Letters from Russia, 1917–19," *Bulletin of the Missouri Historical Society* 14, no. 2 (January 1958): 142.

31. *Na fronte imperialisticheskoi voiny* (Moscow, 1935), pp. 35–36.

32. V. Maklakov, "Tragicheskoe polozhenie," *Russkiya vedomosti*, 27 September 1915, p. 2.

33. Robert Paul Browder and Alexander F. Kerensky, *The Russian Provisional Government, 1917: Documents*, 3 vols. (Stanford, California: Stanford University Press, 1961), vol. 1, p. 17. (Hereafter cited as Browder and Kerensky.)

34. Robert Tucker, *The Lenin Anthology* (New York: W. W. Norton & Co., 1975), p. 292.

35. V. Zenzinov, "Fevral'skie dni," *Novyi zhurnal* 34 (1953): 200–01.

36. O. A. Chaadaeva, "Soldatskie pis'ma v gody mirovoi voiny," *Krasnyi arkhiv*, 65–66 (1934): 158, 142.

37. S. Mstislavsky, *Pyat' dnei: Nachalo i konets fevral'skoi revolyutsii* (Berlin, 1922), p. 12.

38. Browder and Kerensky, vol. 1, p. 36.

39. P. A. Sorokin, *Leaves from a Russian Diary and Thirty Years After* (Boston: Beacon Press, 1950), p. 6.

40. I. Gordienko, *Iz boevogo proshlogo* (Moscow, 1957), p. 58.

41. Browder and Kerensky, vol. 1, p. 38.

42. N. N. Sukhanov, *The Russian Revolution 1917*, edited, abridged, and translated by Joel Carmichael (Princeton, New Jersey: Princeton University Press, 1984), p. 21. (Hereafter cited as Sukhanov.)

43. *Izvestiya Petrogradskogo Soveta rabochikh i soldatskikh deputatov*, no. 32, 4 April 1917.

44. Victor Chernov, *The Great Russian Revolution* (New Haven: Yale University Press, 1936), pp. 172–73.

45. Sukhanov, pp. 192–93.

46. Ibid., p. 72.

47. Shul'gin, *Dni*, p. 178.

48. Sukhanov, p. 53.

49. Ibid., p. 145.

50. Gorky goes on to note: "my correspondents, pretending to be ignorant, insist that all Jews are anarchists. This is a rotten generalization. I am convinced, I know that most of the Jews, to my surprise, manifest more intelligent love for Russia than do many Russians. . . . Idiocy is an illness that cannot be cured by suggestion. For the person stricken with this incurable illness it is clear that since seven and a half Bolsheviks happen to be Jews, the Jewish people are to blame for everything." Maxim Gorky, *Untimely Thoughts: Essays on Revolution, Culture, and the Bolsheviks, 1917–1918*, trans. Herman Ermolaev (New York: Paul S. Eriksson, 1968), pp. 60–62.

51. Ibid., p. 15.

52. Claude Anet, *Through the Russian Revolution: Notes of an Eye-Witness, from 12th March–30th May* (London: Hutchinson & Co., 1917), p. 105.

53. *Velikaya Oktyabr'skaya sotsialisticheskaya revolyutsiya. Dokumenty i materialy: Revolyutsionnoe dvizhenie v Rossii posle sverzheniya samoderzhaviya* (Moscow, 1957), p. 465.

54. *Rabochaya gazeta*, as quoted in David Mandel, *The Petrograd Workers and the Fall of the Old Regime* (New York: St. Martin's Press, 1983), p. 113.

55. As quoted in Richard Abraham, *Alexander Kerensky: The First Love of the Revolution* (New York: Columbia University Press, 1987), p. 199.

56. Florence Farmbourough, *Nurse at the Russian Front* (London: Futura Publications, 1977), pp. 269–70.

57. Abraham, *Alexander Kerensky*, p. 207.

58. Sukhanov, p. 33.

59. Ibid., p. 280.

60. As quoted in Chamberlin, *Russian Revolution*, vol. 1, p. 121.

61. As quoted in Tucker, *Lenin*, p. xlvi.

62. Ibid., p. 301.

63. I. G. Tsereteli, *Vospominaniya o fevral'skoi revolyutsii* (Paris: Mouton, 1963), vol. 1, p. 130. Emphasis added.

64. Browder and Kerensky, vol. 2, p. 942.

65. Ibid., p. 963.

66. *Izvestiya vybornykh sovetov osoboi armii*, 8 June 1917; Alexander Kerensky, *Russia and History's Turning Point* (New York: Duell, Sloan and Pearce, 1965), p. 282.

67. See Sukhanov, pp. 444–47; Alexander Rabinowitch, *Prelude to Revolution: The Petrograd Bolsheviks and the July 1917 Uprising* (Bloomington, Indiana: Indiana University Press, 1968), pp. 152–54.

68. N. N. Sukhanov, *Zapiski o revolyutsii*, 7 vols. (Berlin, 1922–23), vol. 4, pp. 430–31.

69. Gorky, *Untimely Thoughts*, p. 72.

70. Sukhanov, p. 470.

71. *Zhurnaly zasedanii Vremennogo pravitel'stva*, 6 July 1917, p. 1.

72. *Novaya zhizn'*, 18 July 1917, p. 1.

73. Donald J. Raleigh, *Revolution on the Volga: 1917 in Saratov* (Ithaca, New York: Cornell University Press, 1986), p. 186.

74. Sukhanov, p. 533.

75. Sukhanov, *Zapiski o revolyutsii*, vol. 5, pp. 291–92.

76. John Reed, *Ten Days That Shook the World* (New York: Vintage, 1960), p. lvi.

77. Sukhanov, p. 530.

78. E. N. Gorodetsky, *Rozhdenie sovetskogo gosudarstva, 1917–1918* (Moscow, 1965), p. 117.

79. D. Anin, *Revolyutsiya 1917 glazami ee rukovoditelei* (Rome: Edizioni Aurora, 1971), pp. 365, 367.

80. Lenin, *Polnoe sobranie sochinenii*, 55 vols., 5th ed., (Moscow: 1958–65), vol. 34, pp. 280–83.

81. Gorky, *Untimely Thoughts*, p. 83.

82. *Izvestiya*, 25 October 1917, p. 3.

83. Sukhanov, p. 583.

84. As quoted in Alexander Rabinowitch, *The Bolsheviks Come to Power: The Revolution of 1917 in Petrograd* (New York: W. W. Norton, 1976), p. 245.

85. Sukhanov, p. 596.

86. Sukhanov, p. 614.

87. Reed, *Ten Days*, pp. 75, 77.

88. Robert V. Daniels, *Red October: The Bolshevik Revolution of 1917* (New York: Charles Scribner's Sons, 1967), p. 161.

89. Lenin, *Polnoe sobranie sochinenii*, vol. 35, p. 1.

90. Reed, *Ten Days*, pp. 138–39.

91. A. F. Butenko and D. A. Chugaev, eds., *Vtoroi vserossiiskii s''ezd sovetov rabochikh i soldatskikh deputatov: Sbornik dokumentov* (Moscow, 1957), pp. 43–44.

92. Boris Pasternak, *Dr. Zhivago*, trans. Max Hayward and Manya Harari (New York: Pantheon, 1958). Reprint (New York: Signet, n.d.), p. 124.

93. Gorky, *Untimely Thoughts*, pp. 83, 95.

94. Sorokin, *Leaves from a Russian Diary*, p. 103.

95. Lenin to Dzerzhinsky, in James Bunyan and H. H. Fisher, *The Bolshevik Revolution, 1917–1918: Documents and Materials* (Stanford, California: Stanford University Press, 1934), p. 297.

96. Reed, *Ten Days*, p. 380.

NOTE TO THE PHOTOGRAPHS

Most of the photographs on the following pages were taken by professional photographers. When the photographer's name is known, it is given in the caption. The cameras they used were large and required cumbersome glass negatives that shattered easily. Cracks in the glass can be seen on some of the photographs printed from the original negatives.

A number of factors hampered the photographer's task in 1917. Supplies from abroad, especially from Germany, were hard to come by because of the war. Peasant unrest discouraged photographers from venturing out into the countryside. Fear of the peasants caused noblemen landowners to flee their estates; the few who remained were understandably reluctant to pull out cameras and start documenting "criminal" actions against their property. As a result, photographs of peasants—the great majority of the population—are underrepresented.

Then, as now, journalists and photographers felt compelled to stay in the big cities and record major political events as they unfolded. Those photographers who had smaller, more portable cameras attempted to capture spontaneous, "critical" moments, sometimes at great personal risk. The photographer in the picture on this page was arrested for his suspected sympathies toward the insurgents. French journalist Claude Anet tried to take pictures of troops going over to the side of the Revolution in February:

"It was an astonishing sight. Urged on by the sentiment of professional duty, I decided to secure some photographs of these revolutionary scenes, and I went up to my room to fetch my camera. Concealed behind a motor-car, I took, with due precaution, three photographs of the regiment. . . . Then, having hidden my camera in my pocket, I turned towards my door. But I had been observed. Three soldiers rushed upon me and pinned me to the wall, holding their three bayonets against my chest. . . . It was about time for this ridiculous scene to terminate and a tall rascal, who had thrown a military cloak over his civilian clothes, put an end to it by springing forward, snatching the camera from me and making off with it."*

Such conditions forced a kind of self-censorship and caution that limited the range of the photographs taken. Moreover, many pictures did not survive the subsequent whirlwind of events: civil war, collectivization, the purges, World War II. Nevertheless, the examples that appear on these pages testify to the remarkable courage and talent of some of the photographers, as well as to the care of Soviet archivists who so lovingly preserved documents that bring the human struggle of revolution alive again and again.

*Claude Anet, *Through the Russian Revolution: Notes of an Eye-Witness, from 12th March–30th May* (London: Hutchinson & Co., 1917), pp. 18–19.

Russia greeted the New Year, 1917, with a deep sense of foreboding. Three years of world war had inflicted grave hardships on the country. Food and fuel were in critically short supply. With millions of men away at the front, working-class women were taking on more and more of the factory jobs. The gulf between the increasingly overburdened proletariat and the privileged classes was becoming wider than ever before; workers lived in cramped barracks and ate in squalor, while the nobility dined in luxury. Poor leadership and corruption were plaguing the war effort and the patriotic spirit that had unified the country at the beginning of the war was wearing thin. Even the people's traditional faith in the tsar was shaken when he left the capital, Petrograd, to lead the army at the front and entrusted the running of the government to his wife, the German-born Alexandra. The Duma, Russia's quasi-parliament, could do little but talk, and not very boldly at that. The apprehension gripping the country was perhaps best summed up by the governor of Tula province when he wrote: "Such terrible times have set in that I don't know how to cope. Food supplies are in a very bad state, nothing is being brought in, there are lines everywhere. . . . I am sitting on a powder keg."

On the eve of a tumultuous year, the rituals of daily life continue unchanged. A well-to-do woman and her daughter select a New Year's tree.

RUSSIA 1917

JANUARY

ЯНВАРЬ

The air is full of electricity and one
feels the approach of a
thunderstorm. No one can tell
where or when the first thunderclap
will occur. . . .

—PAVEL MILIUKOV, DECEMBER 1916

The harsh conditions of the war's fourth winter do not keep Russians indoors.

ABOVE

Trams crammed with ■ soldiers, schoolboys in uniform, and office workers.

RIGHT

Sleigh drivers look for ■ fares in the crowd strolling on Palace Square in front of the Winter Palace, Petrograd.

RIGHT INSET

Pedestrians and horse- ■ drawn cabs promenade along the capital's great avenue, Nevsky Prospect.

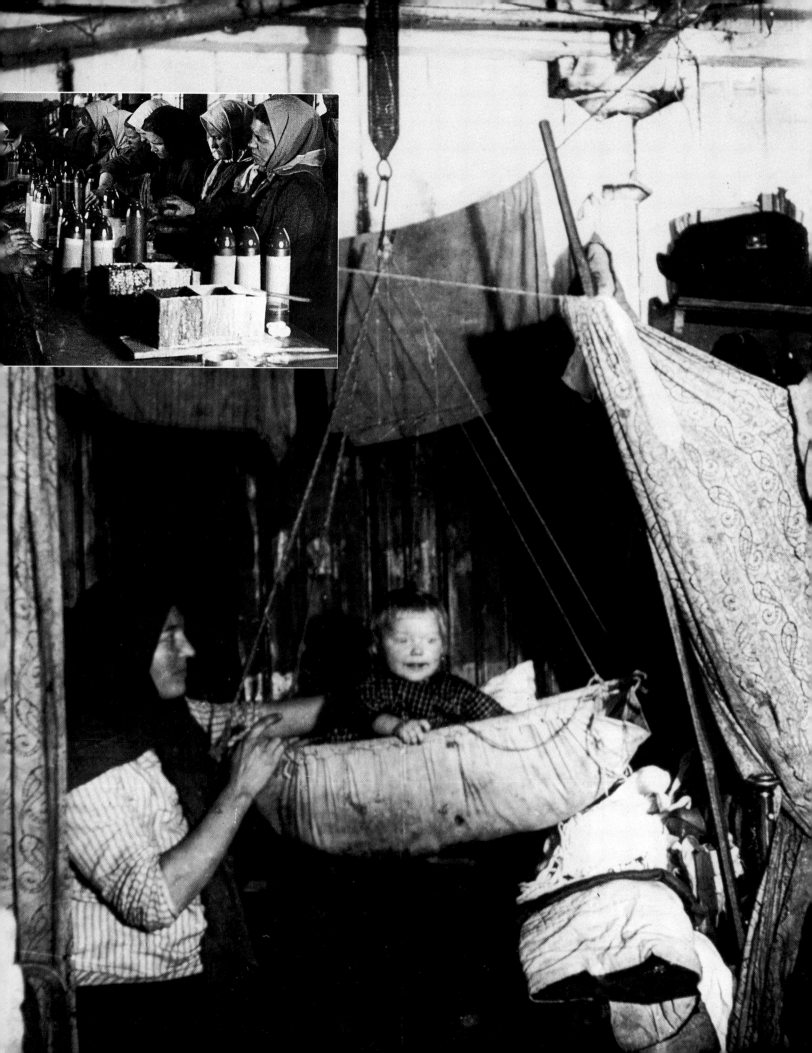

Soldiers at the front greet
■ the New Year in their
trenches.
LEFT

Workers' barracks are
■ crowded and primitive,
but not without basic joys.
LEFT INSET

The war industry,
■ desperate for laborers,
brings thousands of women
into munitions factories.

In an economy of guns or butter, even the highly skilled, well-paid metalworkers who make artillery pieces have little to buy with their wages.
LEFT

Everything for the front. Workers turn out thousands of shells.
BELOW

Coal miners work to heat the capital and fuel supply trains to the front.

Opportunities for women
office workers, such as
jobs at the telephone
exchange—Petrograd's nerve
center for information and
rumors—grow as the war
takes the men away.

The social gulf that was an underlying cause of the Revolution.

ABOVE

A workers' eating hall.
■

RIGHT

A dinner for the nobility at
■ Prince Shakhovskoy's.

ABOVE

Duma chairman Mikhail Rodzyanko (1859–1924).

RIGHT

Rodzyanko presides over one of the last meetings of the Fourth Duma in the Tauride Palace, Petrograd. The tsarina referred to this group as "the loathsome Rodzyanko and those other creatures."

The privations of war and the unequal distribution of its burdens fueled the politics of resentment. Women workers in Petrograd had to cope with more than 200% inflation. Their rallies to commemorate International Women's Day, 23 February (old style) quickly turned into demonstrations demanding "Bread!" Events then snowballed spontaneously; it took no conspiratorial planning by revolutionary parties to convince workers long fed up with inequities to take to the streets demanding "Down with the monarchy!" Soon the troops stationed in the capital refused orders to defend the tsarist status quo and they too went over to the side of the Revolution. Carrying their revolutionary icons—banners of freedom—people gravitated to the seat of oppositional authority, the Tauride Palace, where the Duma had its headquarters and the Soviet of Workers' Deputies was formed. News of the Revolution spread around the country from there. Crowds attacked the hated bastions of the old regime: police headquarters, jails, and archives where the secret police stored their records. If the Revolution was to fail, the men and women in the streets wanted to make it as difficult as possible for the organs of repression to resume their work. But to everyone's surprise the Revolution succeeded. The 300-year-old Romanov regime was overthrown and a new democratic Russia was born.

The Revolution's humble beginnings. Petrograd's women workers demonstrating on 23 February. The banner proclaims: "Increase Rations for Soldiers' Families, the Defenders of Freedom and a People's Peace."

RUSSIA
1917

FEBRUARY

ФЕВРАЛЬ

Out of the way, obsolete world,
rotten from top to bottom. Young
Russia is on the march!

Insurrection quickly spreads.

LEFT INSET

Street barricades outside
■ the Sergievskaya
Pharmacy, corner of
Sergievskaya Street and
Liteiny Prospect, Petrograd.

LEFT

Soldiers demonstrating on
■ Nevsky Prospect near the
Catherine Garden.

BELOW

Demonstration against the
■ war on Liteiny Prospect.
Photo K. Bulla.

TOP

Tank Corps members go over to the Revolution. Chalked on their vehicle: "Freedom!/28 February/ Tank Division/1917."

BOTTOM

Hastily formed people's militia arresting former police officers. Photo Ya. Steinberg.

RIGHT

Revolutionaries firing on Petrograd police headquarters.

Revolutionary leaflets
■ being distributed,
28 February.

LEFT

A demonstration outside
■ the Tauride Palace,
where the Duma met from
1906 to 1917. Photo Ya.
Steinberg.

LEFT INSET

On 27 February workers
■ and soldiers of the newly
formed Petrograd Soviet
meet in the Tauride Palace
for the first time.

Insurgent soldiers of
the Preobrazhensky
Regiment, one of the first to
go over to the Revolution,
stationed in the Catherine
Hall of the Tauride Palace.

RIGHT

Soldiers and officers of the
Petrograd garrison, who
participated in overthrowing
autocracy, pose for
photographer K. Bulla. The
banner reads: "Down with
the Monarchy! Long Live
the Democratic Republic!"

The Revolution spreads to
Moscow.

ABOVE

The insurrection begins on
■ Tverskaya (now Gorky)
Street.

RIGHT

Muscovites reading the first
■ news of the Revolution.

In Petrograd revolutionaries
destroy bastions of tsarist
power to thwart a return to
autocracy.

LEFT

The house of preliminary
detention is ransacked
and all political prisoners
are freed.

TOP RIGHT

The Petrograd
Correctional Prison,
located in the Lithuanian
Castle, is torched. Photo
K. Bulla.

CENTER RIGHT

In an act as symbolic as it
was practical, the police
archive—the key to secret
police surveillance—is
gutted.

BOTTOM RIGHT

A police station
is razed.

Burning the tsarist coat of arms on Nevsky Prospect, 27 February. Photo K. Bulla.

Revolutionary soldiers encamped in the Winter Palace, the tsar's former residence and now the Hermitage Museum. Canvas covers the parquet floor to protect it from the soldiers' gritty boots.

Iconoclasm: Double-headed eagles, symbol of the Imperial regime, are pulled off the Winter Palace facade.

Vasily V. Shulgin (left), a
■ conservative Duma
member and one of the
two men dispatched to the
front to receive the tsar's
abdication.

RIGHT

The empty throne,
■ St. George Hall,
the Kremlin.

he old order was dead; helter-skelter a new one emerged. A Provisional Government, led by timid liberals, was formed with the acquiescence and cooperation of the Petrograd Soviet of Workers' and Soldiers' Deputies; in effect, a "dual power" arrangement was created. The Soviet, which was loyally supported by the workers and soldiers who had made the February Revolution and had absorbed most of the thousand or so casualties, rushed to protect law and order. In place of the police, a people's militia was formed and Order No. 1, democratizing the armed forces, was issued. Long-suppressed causes and beliefs could now be voiced and paraded in public, and, from Petrograd to Irkutsk, everyone, it seemed, was on the march: the most extreme leftists—the anarchists; women demanding the right to vote; the Jewish Bund; adolescents calling for the abolition of child labor; civil servants demanding an eight-hour workday. The chaos of democracy swiftly replaced the straightjacket of tsarist repression. And long-exiled political leaders, Lenin among them, headed home to participate in the realization of a free Russia.

The February Revolution ▪ rekindles national pride and a renewed dedication to fighting the war, as this banner, "War to a Victorious End," proclaims.

MARCH

МАРТЪ

It was felt, and for the first time, that the Russian people, yes, the Russian people, had made a revolution. It rose from the dead to join the great cause of the world— the building of new and ever-so- free forms of life.

—MAXIM GORKY

Sailors on the cruiser ■ *Riurik* adopt the Revolution's egalitarianism by slicing off the epaulets emblematic of the old regime's system of rank and privilege.

RIGHT

Signing up for the people's ■ militia at the Tauride Palace. The man in the center holds copies of "Order No. 1," which democratized the armed services.

ВЪ ДЕНЬ ПРАЗДНИКА РЕВОЛЮЦІИ /ІІІ 1917г. АРТ. ДУРОВЪ ХОРОНИТЪ СТАРЫЙ РЕЖИМЪ. НА ГРОБЪ СИДЯТ ПРОТОПОПОВЪ и РАСПУТИНЪ. 39.

Dismantling the old order.
TOP TO BOTTOM

A soldier pries the double-headed eagle from a building.

Tsarist emblems on the Winter Palace fence are draped in black.

The tsar's personal car, inventively equipped for winter with skis and tracks, is nationalized. It stands in front of the Ministry of Justice on Italyanskaya Street at Minister of Justice Kerensky's disposal.

A 1917 "happening": The artist Durov celebrates the "holiday of the Revolution," 12 March, by staging the funeral of the old regime. Seated on the "coffin" of the old regime are "Rasputin" and his candidate for minister of justice, "Protopopov."

RIGHT

Soldiers from the Pavlovsky Regiment reading about the tsar's abdication in the newspaper *Izvestiya* (News).

RIGHT INSET

Revolutionary guards line the hall of the Tauride Palace leading to the room where arrested tsarist ministers are held.

The February Revolution
was not bloodless. Petrograd
authorities listed 1,224
individuals killed or
wounded.

Bodies of the Revolution's
■ victims are readied for
burial, 23 March.

A solemn ceremony down
■ Nevsky Prospect honors
those fallen in the name of
freedom. The banner reads:
"You Fell Victim. . . ."

The fallen heroes are
■ buried in Petrograd's
Field of Mars.

Representatives of the Petrograd garrison gather to honor their fallen brothers on the Field of Mars. The banners proclaim: "Eternal and Glorious Memory to Our Comrades—Fighters for Freedom"; "Long Live the Democratic Republic."

Establishing a new order.
TOP

The commandant of the Tauride Palace hands out passes to the people.

BOTTOM

Izvestiya of the Petrograd Soviet being distributed to representatives of army units. Photo Ya. Steinberg.

RIGHT

A meeting of the Soviet of Soldiers' Deputies in the Tauride Palace. Photo V. Bulla.

In demonstrations all over Russia, the people show their support of the new regime.

TOP LEFT

In front of the Metropole ■ Hotel, Moscow, 12 March. The banners state: "Long Live a Free Russia"; "Long Live the Democratic Republic. Long Live the International!"

BOTTOM LEFT

In Petrograd, soldiers ■ carry a banner that reads: "Long Live the Soviet of Workers' and Soldiers' Deputies. Long Live the Provisional Government in Agremeent with It."

TOP RIGHT

In Kiev, the militia of the ■ local Soviet of Workers' Deputies take part in a parade.

CENTER RIGHT

A demonstration in Irkutsk, ■ Siberia.

BOTTOM RIGHT

In Kharkov, white-collar ■ civil servants demonstrate. The banner of the Employees Union of All Government Institutions in Kharkov proclaims: "Long Live Freedom, Equality, and Brotherhood!"

A meeting of soldiers at the
■ front.

LEFT

A parade of troops through
■ Red Square, Moscow,
12 March.

Dual authority emerges.

TOP LEFT

Workers and soldiers ■ outside the Tauride Palace voice their support for the new order. Their banner reads: "Long Live a Nationwide Socialist Republic." Photo K. Bulla.

BOTTOM LEFT

Soldiers of the Keksgolm ■ Regiment take an oath of allegiance to the Provisional Government.

TOP RIGHT

A meeting of the executive ■ committee of the Petrograd Soviet. Seated second from left is Chairman Nikolai Chkheidze.

BOTTOM RIGHT

A photograph of the ■ Provisional Government cabinet of ministers, mistakenly including F. I. Rodichev, who was not, in fact, in the new government. Counterclockwise from left: Prince G. E. Lvov (premier), A. I. Konovalov, A. F. Kerensky, A. I. Guchkov, V. N. Lvov, P. N. Miliukov, M. I. Tereshchenko, F. I. Rodichev, N. V. Nekrasov, A. A. Manuilov, A. I. Shingarev, I. V. Godnev.

Кн. Г. Е. Львовъ, А. И. Коноваловъ, А. Ф. Керенскій. А. И. Гучковъ, В. Н. Львовъ, П. Н. Милюковъ, М. И. Терещенко, Ф. И. Родичевъ, Н. В. Некрасовъ, А. А. Мануиловъ, А. И. Шингаревъ, И. В. Годневъ.

Russia's many
■revolutionary parties
emerge from the
underground. Here a
demonstration of the
Socialist Revolutionary
party on Nevsky Prospect.

Members of the Jewish Bund stop for a photograph. Their banner, in Russian and Yiddish, reads: "Long Live the Universal Jewish Workers Union, 'The Bund.' Long Live the International Proletariat!"

Women demand their rights.

TOP LEFT

Women demonstrating
■ on Nevsky Prospect in
front of Gostinny Dvor,
Petrograd's great shopping
arcade, 19 March. Viewed
from photographer K. Bulla's
studio window.

BOTTOM LEFT

Detail of the same
■ demonstration. The
banners state: "Russian
League for the Equality of
Women"; "Electoral Rights
for Women!"

TOP RIGHT

Working women demand
■ "Land Rights for Peasant
Women."

CENTER RIGHT

Middle-class women with
■ roses.

BOTTOM RIGHT

The banner declares: "If
■ Women Are Slaves There
Won't Be Freedom. Long
Live the Equality of
Women!"

Soldiers rally to defend the new order; workers demand social reforms.

TOP LEFT

Soldiers from Petrograd's ■ armored-car division proclaim: "Tankists for Freedom."

CENTER LEFT

Workers of the ■ Shaposhnikov Tobacco Factory march on Nevsky Prospect.

BOTTOM LEFT

"**G**et the Shells Ready," ■ tankists' banners warn. "The Enemy Is at Our Doorstep."

RIGHT

Adolescents demand an ■ end to child labor and call for an eight-hour workday.

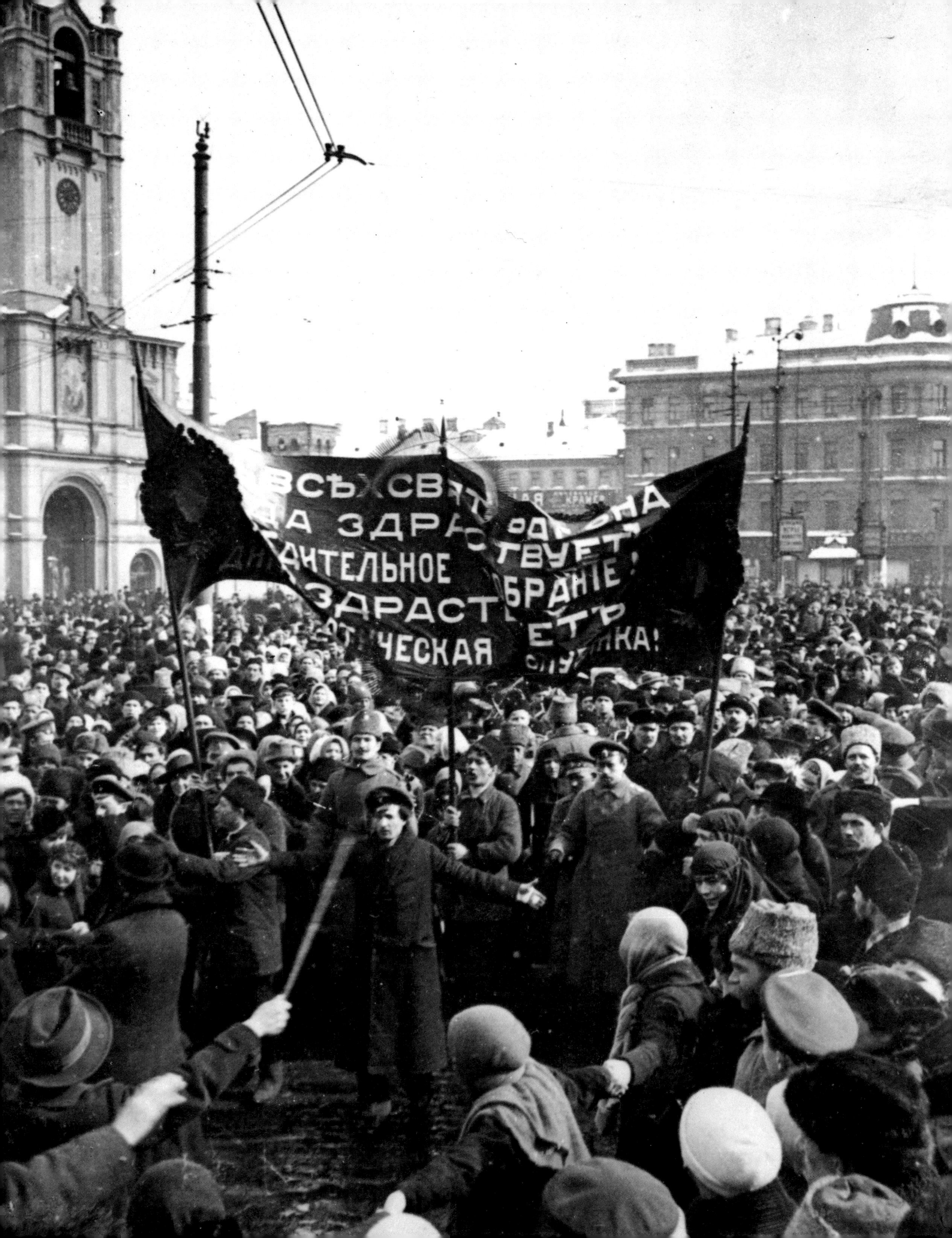
ВСЪ СВЯТ
ДА ЗДРА
ТВУЕТ
ТЕЛЬНОЕ
БРАНIЕ
ЗДРАСТ
ЧЕСКАЯ

Soldiers and sailors gather
■ in the Catherine Hall of
the Tauride Palace. Photo
V. Bulla.

Demonstrators on
■ Strastnaya Square,
Moscow, clamoring for the
convocation of the
Constituent Assembly.

Soldiers on the road to Tsarskoe Selo, where the former tsar and his family were exiled after the February Revolution.

LEFT

A demonstration of school children in Tsarskoe Selo, 24 March. The banners read: "Free High Schools!"; "Long Live Public Education"; "Long Live Autonomous Schools for the Good of the People"; "In Unity There is Strength."

On the road to Finland Station.

ABOVE

A group of exiled
■ Bolsheviks, including
Yakov Sverdlov (center), in
Siberia before their release.

RIGHT

Lenin (with umbrella,
■ right) in Stockholm,
31 March, on his way
home.

By the second full month of the new Russia's life, news of the Revolution had penetrated into the countryside. The peasants took stock of the political revolution in far-off Petrograd and began demanding an overthrow of the old order in the villages. In some locales they sacked manor houses, seized noblemen's firewood, and drove landowners into the cities. These actions instilled a great fear that the privileged beneficiaries of the old regime were about to be slaughtered by the "dark forces" of the peasantry. Because the Russian calendar was thirteen days behind the Western world's calendar, the Russian working class held its first unfettered celebration of May Day on 18 April. Banners calling for socialism and the transformation of the workers' political victory into a social one, floated across scores of Russian cities. The Provisional Government, meanwhile, was pursuing the tsarist government's foreign policy. When Foreign Minister Pavel Miliukov's endorsement of secret Romanov treaties to annex the Dardanelles became public, the news provoked the Provisional Government's first crisis, inciting massive demonstrations and bringing the Soviet into direct conflict with the government. This confrontation highlighted the precarious nature of dual power; it forced Miliukov's resignation and brought about the formation of a "second" Provisional Government.

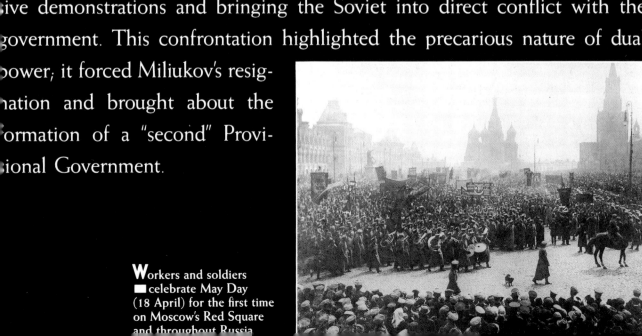

Workers and soldiers celebrate May Day (18 April) for the first time on Moscow's Red Square and throughout Russia

RUSSIA
1917

APRIL

АПРѢЛЬ

The realist is one who can inject
into the social revolution the
greatest number of ideas about
freedom and can make these ideas
not a luxury but a necessity for
the masses.

—YUDA ROSHCHIN

At a meeting in the Dobrovitsyn village church, Orel Province, on 3 April, the peasants pass a resolution to transfer the gentry's land into their own hands.

May Day (18 April)
demonstrations in
Petrograd.

LEFT INSET

In front of the Stock
■ Exchange.

LEFT

On Nevsky Prospect in
■ front of Gostinny Dvor.

ABOVE

Demonstrators marching
■ across the Troitsky
(now Kirov) Bridge toward
the Winter Palace. Photo
K. Bulla.

RIGHT

A speaker at a meeting on
■ St. Isaac's Square. Photo
V. Bulla.

May Day demonstrators converge on Palace Square, Petrograd.

TOP LEFT

The Northern Union of Gardeners. Their banner reads: "Free Science in Support of Free Labor." Photo Ya. Steinberg.

CENTER LEFT

The banner on the left reads: "Long Live the Democratic Republic!" On the right: "Long Live Socialism. United Workers' Trade Institute."

BOTTOM LEFT

On Morskaya Street representatives of the Social Democratic Workers Party of the Psycho-Nerve Institute pose for photographer V. Bulla. "Proletarians of All Countries, Unite!" their banner proclaims. "Long Live the International! Long Live International Peace. . . ."

TOP RIGHT

Palace Square. Photo V. Bulla.

BOTTOM RIGHT

Employees of the National Mint declare: "Long Live the International Holiday of Labor. Long Live Socialism."

FOLLOWING PAGES

May Day parades around the country. Top left: Vladivostok, Siberia. Bottom left: Sumy, the Ukraine. Top right: Kirensk, Siberia. Bottom right: Dvinsk (now Daugavpils), Latvia.

ДА ЗДРАВСТВУЕТЪ
3 й
ИНТЕРНАЦIОНАЛЪ
ДА ЗДРАВСТВУЕТЪ
ДА ЗДРАВСТВУЕТЪ
РОССIЯ
НАРОДЪ
3 ИНТЕРНАЦIОНАЛЪ
УЧЕНИКИ
Н.Р.

Teenage workers from the ■ Putilov Factory take part in the May Day demonstrations. One of their many banners reads: "Adolescents of the Train-Car Division. Long Live Socialism! Freedom, Equality, and Brotherhood." Note the Sunday dress of these radical members of the proletariat.

The April Crisis.

Minister of Foreign Affairs ■ Pavel Miliukov, who urged the Provisional Government to follow the tsarist war program and annex the Dardanelles.

The angry masses take to ■ the streets to protest the policies of "Miliukov-Dardanelsky."

As the winter snows and early spring mud gave way to dry, balmy weather, the peasants began to take action. Everywhere collective meetings sprang up at which they voiced grievances dating back to the abolition of serfdom. Popular justice called for a "black repartition"—the immediate abolition of land as private property and the redistribution of all land to those who worked it. Peasant feelings, first articulated publically during the 1905 Revolution, were reiterated at the first All-Russian Congress of Soviets of Peasants' Deputies: "Land is like air, it should not be bought or sold." The Provisional Government, however, was concentrating its efforts on the war and insisted on putting off all question of social revolution "for the duration" or until a Constituent Assembly could be convened. Representatives of the allied powers came to Russia to see for themselves the results of the long-discussed revolution, but also to insure that Russia remained in the war. It was becoming increasingly difficult and costly for the Provisional Government to wage an unsuccessful and once again unpopular war. As rumors spread that peasant assemblies were taking it upon themselves to redistribute land, soldiers began deserting the front for their native villages.

A food line, Petrograd. ■ With the war still raging, the Provisional Government cannot address pressing domestic issues. (Photograph printed from a cracked glass negative.)

RUSSIA 1917

MAY

МАЙ

The right of private ownership of land is abolished forever. . . . All land is to be taken over without compensation as the property of all the people and given over to the use of whose who work it.

—RESOLUTION OF THE FIRST ALL-RUSSIAN CONGRESS OF PEASANTS' DEPUTIES

Delegates to the First All-Russian Congress of Peasants' Deputies (4–28 May).
LEFT

A peasant meeting in a village.
LEFT INSET

First All-Russian Congress of Peasants' Deputies, Petrograd. One banner proclaims: "Land & Freedom," the traditional slogan of radical populism.

Workers' children relaxing
■ at a special summer
camp for offspring of the
proletariat outside
Petrograd.

RIGHT

A group of students
■ demonstrating for "Free
Public Education" in
Petrograd.

Да Здравствуетъ
Безплатное Народное
Образованіе
г.У. Анг. 34

Russia's allies, Britain and France, anxious for Russia to stay in the war, send representatives to Petrograd.

William Sanders (third from right), British Labor Party member, meeting with Sergeant Kirpichnikov (third from left) and other soldiers of the Volynsky Regiment.

William Sanders speaking at ■ a wreath-laying ceremony, in honor of the victims of the February Revolution, on the Field of Mars.

For some, life goes on as before.

TOP

Women in a cafe.
■

CENTER

Horseback riding on the
■ Neva River embankment,
Petrograd.

BOTTOM

Office clerks taking a
■ break.

For others, hardships increase.

ABOVE

The food distribution center of the Soviet of Workers' and Soldiers' Deputies in the Tauride Palace.

INSET

Lining up for meat on Nechaev Street, Tomsk.

Selling freedom bonds,
■ corner of Nevsky
Prospect and Morskaya
Street. Photo Ya. Steinberg.

Agitating for freedom
■ bonds. Note the
egalitarian gesture of the
officer lighting the sailor's
cigarette.

Soldiers donating their
■ gold medals and St.
George crosses to the
Petrograd Soviet in support
of the revolutionary cause.

Soldiers learning French.
■

Disillusioned with the ■ Provisional Government's handling of the war, many soldiers desert the front.

New recruits are tearfully ■ seen off to the army by their families.

Determined to win the war, to convince the allied powers to keep the financial supply lines open, and to preserve peace at home for the duration, Alexander Kerensky undertook a bold strategy in June: he ordered a summer offensive. He reasoned that an assault all along Russia's fronts would rekindle patriotism and distract the masses from mounting social discontents. Kerensky became the country's agitator-in-chief, encouraging everyone from the Women's Shock Battalion of Death to soldiers stuck in vermin-ridden trenches to do battle in the name of Mother Russia. A charismatic speaker who made powerful, if fleeting, impressions, Kerensky succeeded in inspiring his troops to make one grand charge against the enemy. But he also aroused the anger of his domestic foes, who demanded an end to the war and the expulsion of "capitalists" from the Provisional Government. Many thought the socialist Kerensky had betrayed his beliefs by launching the June offensive. While battles raged he could ignore hecklers on the left, but once the June offensive became the June defeat and casualties reached the thousands, discontents soared. The Provisional Government in Petrograd was teetering dangerously on the brink of military disaster and social revolution.

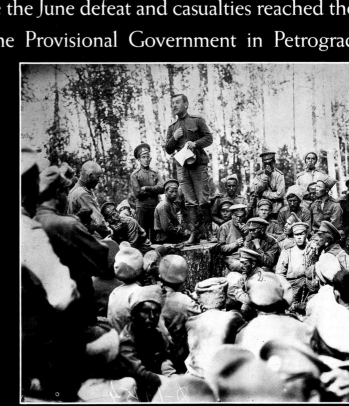

Meeting at the front before an offensive. Morale plummets as Russia suffers defeat after defeat, and soldiers begin to heed the anti-war message of the Bolsheviks and other radical parties.

RUSSIA 1917

JUNE

ИЮНЬ

SOLDIER AT THE FRONT TO KERENSKY:
If there is an offensive, then we shall
all perish and a dead man needs
neither freedom nor land. So the
government should conclude
peace sooner.

KERENSKY:
Tomorrow, order this coward to be
excluded from the ranks of the
Russian army.

The Women's Shock
Battalion of Death.

TOP LEFT

Women soldiers taking a
■ tea break in front of their
tent.

BOTTOM LEFT

Maria Bochkareva,
■ commander of the
women's battalion in 1917.

RIGHT

Members of the women's
■ battalion receiving their
banner and taking the oath
of allegiance before going
off to the front.

TOP RIGHT, INSET

Patriarch Nikon blessing
■ the women's battalion on
Red Square.

BOTTOM RIGHT, INSET

Target practice.
■

The June offensive gets under way. Soldiers departing for the front, Petrograd. The banner reads: "First We'll End the War, Then We'll Get on with Our Lives."

A public church service for the troops on Red Square.

In the trenches on the
■ western front.

Alexander Kerensky, seated
at the former tsar's desk
in the Winter Palace.

Kensky delivering an impassioned speech at the front.

On the eve of the offensive Kerensky's charm and powers of persuasion inspire soldiers to fight for the motherland.

Support for the June offensive comes from unexpected quarters: the Father of Russian Marxism, G. V. Plekhanov (holding Kerensky's portrait), and the white-haired veteran revolutionary, L. G. Deutsch.

General A. A. Brusilov, ■ Kerensky's supreme commander in chief. He later joined the Red Army.

Admiral A. V. Kolchak, ■ commander in chief of the Black Sea Fleet. He later became a leader of the White Army against the Soviet government.

RIGHT

A group of delegates to ■ the First All-Russian Congress of Workers' and Soldiers' Deputies, including Mensheviks N. S. Chkheidze, G. V. Plekhanov, and M. I. Skobelev (first row, second, third, and fourth from right, respectively).

Политическая манифестація 18-го Іюня 1917 г. въ Петроградѣ.

Disillusionment with the Provisional Government's military and social policies grows.

LEFT

A political demonstration in Petrograd, 18 June. The soldiers' banner reads: "Long Live the 3rd International!"

FACING PAGE:

TOP LEFT

At the same demonstration other soldiers demand: "Send Nicholas the Bloody to the Peter and Paul Fortress" (Petrograd's prison for political offenders).

TOP RIGHT

Waiters voice their grievances: "We Demand Respect for the Human Being in a Waiter"; "Down with Tips"; "Long Live the 8-Hour Day for All Employees!"

CENTER

Anti-government demonstrators demand: "Down with the Ten Capitalist Ministers."

BOTTOM LEFT

Workers of the Petrograd Munitions Factory march in support of the Bolsheviks and Anarchists.

BOTTOM RIGHT

Workers' banners indicate their increasing radicalism: "Workers' Control over Production and Distribution of Goods"; "Power to the Soviet of W[orkers'], S[oldiers'], and P[easants'] Deputies"; "Down with the Capitalist Ministers!"

A meeting at the
■ Kshesinskaya mansion,
Bolshevik headquarters until
July. This art nouveau
building had been the home
of the ballerina Mathilde
Kshesinskaya.

BELOW

O rator speaking to striking
■ factory workers.

RIGHT

D emonstrators on Nevsky
■ Prospect, 18 June.
Members of the Bolshevik
Committee of the Liteiny
region carry a banner that
proclaims: "Long Live the
Social Revolution."

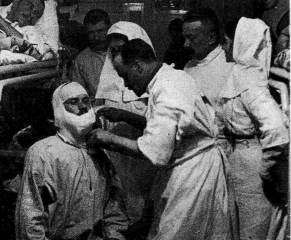

The June offensive fails, taking a deadly toll.

TOP

The wounded await
■ treatment and
evacuation.

BOTTOM

Doctors and nurses
■ minister to the injured.

RIGHT

Bodies of Russian soldiers
■ felled in the line of duty.

FOLLOWING PAGE

Funeral service for soldiers
■ killed in the offensive in
Galicia.

opular anger exploded in early July. Thousands of soldiers, inspired by effective leftist (Bolshevik, Left Socialist Revolutionary, and Anarchist) propaganda, expressed their lack of confidence in the Provisional Government by "voting with their feet." They took their guns and deserted the front. Petrograd became a seething cauldron of working-class fury. Unable to restrain worker hostility, Bolshevik organizers stood by helplessly as men from the factories took to the streets in an incredible display of spontaneous militance and demanded an end to the war, all power to the soviets, and worker control over production. As in February, "the street" seemed poised to make its own revolution. Only this time workers had the experience of February behind them and were well armed. Kerensky's government was in shambles, but he was determined to stay in power at any cost. Troops loyal to him amassed and opened fire on the protesters. Bolshevik and Anarchist headquarters were sacked; the Bolsheviks' newspaper, *Pravda*, was shut down. Trotsky and other Bolshevik leaders were thrown in jail. Lenin shaved his beard and escaped incognito to a hiding place in Finland. Temporarily triumphant in suppressing the rising radical tide, Kerensky became prime minister and formed a new coalition government.

On 4 July soldiers, sailors, and workers take to the streets demanding the immediate overthrow of the Provisional Government. Their demonstration is met with gunfire and many are killed.

RUSSIA
1917

JULY

ИЮЛЬ

The Bolsheviks made every effort to
reduce the July movement to a
demonstration. But did it not,
nevertheless, by the very logic of
things, transcend these limits?

—LEON TROTSKY

After the failed offense, anti-war sentiment explodes.

BELOW

The Bolsheviks' newspaper, ■ *Trench Pravda*, proclaims: "Nations, Extend Your Hands to One Another in Brotherhood."

ABOVE

Members of the radical ■ Latvian rifle regiment reading this great propaganda vehicle.

LEFT

The banners demand: ■ "Peace without Victors"; "Peace without Annexations or Indemnities"; "Down with the Bloody War! Long Live an Immediate Honorable Peace!"; "Forward to a Free Russia"; "Fight Capital"; "Land and Freedom."

LEFT INSET

Soldiers deserting the ■ front.

Popular radicalism reaches its peak on 4 July in a demonstration on Nevsky Prospect.

LEFT, TOP TO BOTTOM

"Down with the Counterrevolution! Down with the 10 Capitalist Ministers! All Power to the Soviets! We Demand the Immediate Convocation of the Constituent Assembly!"

"Workers' Control of Production and Distribution."

"All Power to the Soviet! Down with the Capitalist Ministers! Down with the State Duma!"

"We Demand Immediate Publication of Secret Treaties with the Allies!"

Rebellious sailors and soldiers, in a far more radical mood than their party leaders, call for an overthrow of the government by armed force. Radical sailors loading machine-gun belts. Photo V. Bulla.

Radical soldiers of the first machine-gun regiment.

BELOW

The forces of law and order prepare to defend Kerensky's government. General P. A. Polovtsev with troops summoned from the front to crush "mutinies." Kerensky soon fired him for "indecisiveness."

Tensions mount as forces gather.

ABOVE

The 4 July demonstration
■ continues down Nevsky Prospect. The banners read: "Long Live Socialism!"; "Down with the Capitalist Ministers! All Power to the Soviets!"

RIGHT

The Provisional
■ Government's army assembles in front of the Mariinsky Palace.

RIGHT INSET

Members of the fifth army
■ amass on Palace Square.

FOLLOWING PAGE

Government troops open
■ fire on demonstators at the corner of Nevsky Prospect and Sadovaya Street. Photo V. Bulla.

Consequences of the government's repressive actions.

ABOVE

Although Lenin played a secondary role in July, he was forced to beat an ignominious, albeit temporary, retreat. He shaved his beard and went underground to avoid arrest.

TOP, FAR LEFT

Cossacks surround the body of a horse wounded in the 4 July attack on demonstrators.

CENTER, FAR LEFT

Soldiers of the first machine-gun regiment are disarmed.

BOTTOM, FAR LEFT

A photographer suspected of Bolshevik sympathies is arrested.

LEFT

Soldiers on the staircase of the Kshesinskaya mansion, Bolshevik headquarters, after government troops took control.

After routing leftists in July, Kerensky was intent upon restoring government authority. To strengthen the army and rebuild officer morale, he appointed General Lavr Kornilov, a war hero with a reputation for severity and toughness, as his new commander in chief. As civilians faced increased food shortages and widespread rationing, Kornilov made his plans for saving Russia. He reinstituted the death penalty at the front, called for the abolition of strikes, and demanded the formation of an ironfisted central government that would wrest control from workers and soldiers. Conservatives endorsed Kornilov at a state conference in Moscow, but soon a power struggle erupted. Kerensky and Kornilov, each trying to exploit the other, came to loggerheads. Kornilov tried to seize power by marching on Petrograd with his troops. Workers, who interpreted Kornilov's message as a direct assault on all the freedoms gained since February, marshalled their strength to defend the city and, by extension, Kerensky's government. As if that weren't enough of an irony, Kornilov's troops, when confronted, refused to fight. His counterrevolutionary coup failed. Red Guards, as revolutionary workers' groups were now called, accepted the arms surrendered by the counterrevolutionaries. They would soon have reason to make good use of these weapons.

General Lavr Kornilov's counterrevolutionary coup attempt is squashed by increasingly radical and well-armed workers, soldiers, and peasants.

RUSSIA 1917

AUGUST

АВГУСТЪ

The scoundrel! The upstart! I swear
by the honor of an old soldier that
I do not want tsarism restored. The
idiot! He [Kerensky] can't see that
his days are numbered. . . .
Tomorrow, Lenin will have his head
and everything will be wrecked.

—GENERAL LAVR KORNILOV

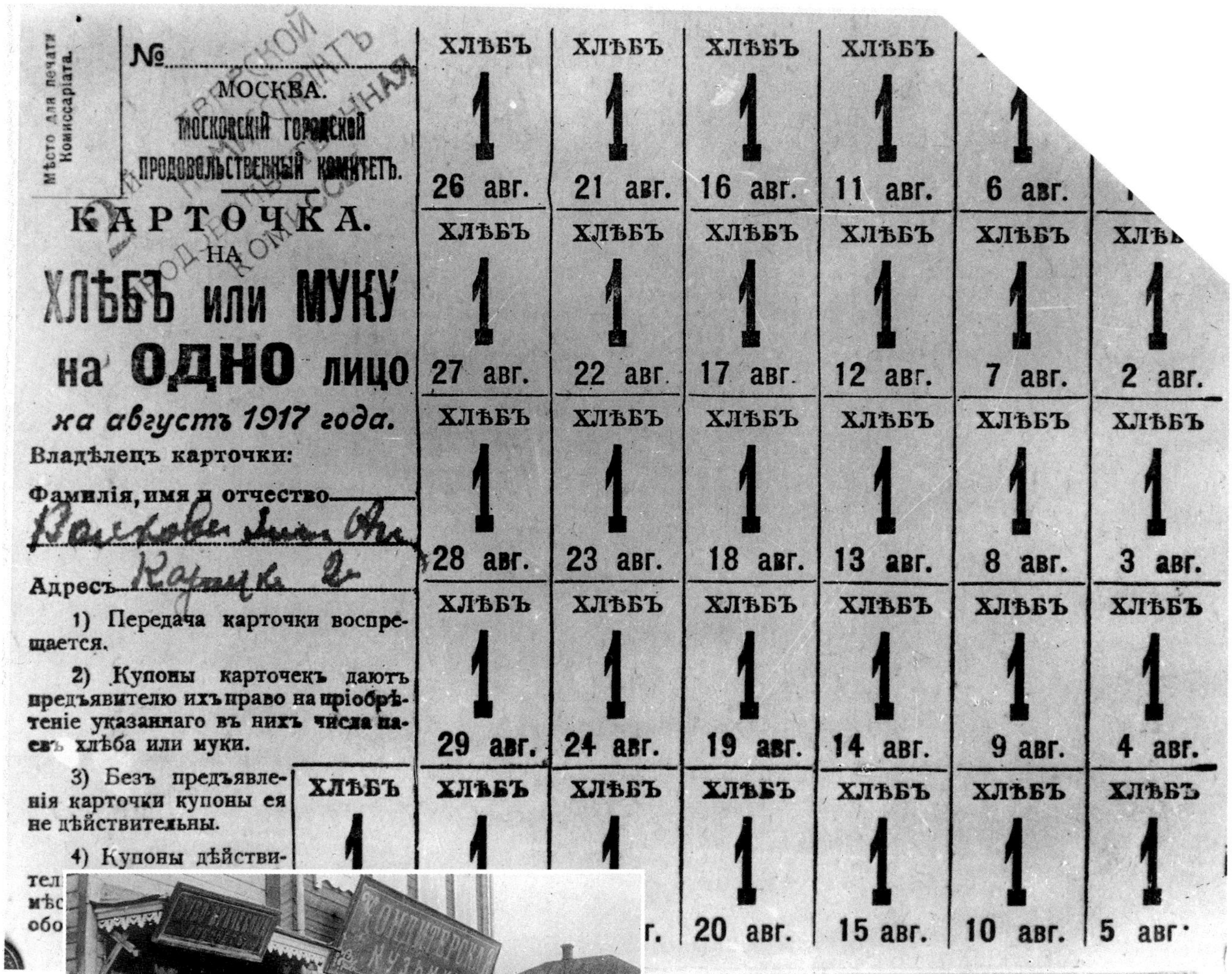

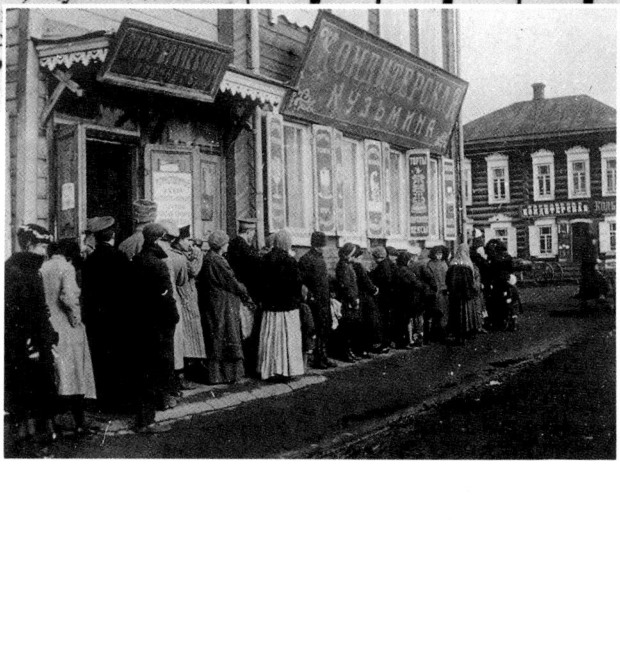

Food shortages lead to
long bread lines (left) and
ration coupons (above). This
is a bread or flour coupon
for one person for the
month of August.

Kerensky's military cabinet
■ in August. Left to right:
General V. L. Baranovsky,
Col. G. Ya. Yakubovich,
B. V. Savinkov, Kerensky,
Prince G. P. Tumanov.

The second coalition
■ government. First row,
left to right: P. P. Yurenev
(transportation), F. F.
Kokoshkin (controller), A. V.
Peshekhonov (food), N. V.
Nekrasov (deputy prime
minister and finance), A. F.
Kerensky (prime minister
and war), N. D. Avksentiev
(interior), V. M. Chernov
(agriculture), A. M. Nikitin
(post and telegraph). Second
row: A. V. Kartashev
(religion), S. F. Oldenburg
(education), A. S. Zarudny
(justice), I. N. Efremov
(welfare), B. V. Savinkov
(deputy war minister), M. I.
Skobelev (labor), S. N.
Prokopovich (industry and
commerce).

ABOVE

General Lavr Kornilov,
whom Kerensky
appointed as the new
commander in chief.

LEFT

The Bolshoi Theater,
Moscow, where the State
Conference was held, 12–15
August.

BELOW

Foreign dignitaries
attending the State
Conference.

General Kornilov, a brave,
■ respected disciplinarian,
addressing his troops.
BELOW LEFT

Some of Kornilov's
■ soldiers, ready to fight to
the death.
BELOW CENTER ˙

Representatives of
■ Kornilov's Wild Division
conducting truce
negotiations. Standing in the
center is Cossack Sergeant
Hadji Murat Dzarakokhov
of the Tatar regiment. Photo
Ya. Steinberg.
BELOW RIGHT

People in Tomsk reading a
■ telegram about the
Kornilov mutiny.
RIGHT

The Muslim battalion of
■ Kornilov's Wild Division.

Всерос. Центр. Исп. Ком. Сов. Раб. и Сол. Деп.

Кто за Корнилова - тотъ противъ революціи.

Кто противъ революціи - тотъ противъ народа.

Кто противъ народа - тотъ противъ спасенія родины.

Безъ народа - нѣтъ спасенія родины!

Staff headquarters for the
■ fight against Kornilov,
Tsarskoe Selo.

BELOW

Armed workers marching
■ to head off a Kornilov
attack on Petrograd.

LEFT

Leaflet distributed by
■ the Soviet's Executive
Committee: "Those who
are for Kornilov are against
the revolution. Those
against the revolution

are against the people.
Those against the people are
against the salvation of the
motherland. Without the
people there is no salvation
of the motherland!"

A Red Guards' post.
■

Kornilov's men fraternizing
■ with soldiers from the
Petrograd garrison who
accepted their surrender.
Photo Ya. Steinberg.

Disarming Kornilov's
■ troops.

Autumn brought a rising tide of radicalism. The failed June offensive, the July attacks on Anarchist and Bolshevik headquarters, General Kornilov's abortive counterrevolution in August, and the ever worsening food shortage all fed a militant spirit. Elections to the Petrograd and Moscow Dumas (organs of local self-government) produced major gains for the Bolsheviks. In new elections to the Petrograd Soviet, the Bolsheviks won a majority for the first time and Leon Trotsky, now a Bolshevik, became its chairman. No longer would the Soviet tolerate compromise with the Provisional Government; the two parts of the dual-power arrangement were on a collision course. Bolshevik speakers and propaganda struck highly responsive chords in workers and soldiers. The masses' aspirations and fears were echoed in the Bolsheviks' simple, direct, and highly effective slogans—"Peace, Bread, Land"; "All Power to the Soviets!"—that can be seen on banners in so many photographs. Lenin, though still in hiding in Finland, was acutely aware of the growing desperation in the food lines and the increasing militance in the factories, and he exhorted the Bolsheviks' Central Committee to take up his initiative and prepare for an armed overthrow of the Provisional Government.

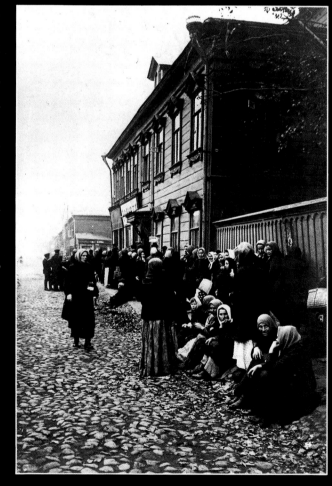

Food shortages continue to plague the country and women wait in ever longer lines.

SEPTEMBER

СЕНТЯБРЬ

Trotsky had been released from
prison on September 4th. . . . Now
he became chairman of the
Petrograd Soviet; there was a
hurricane of applause when he
appeared. Everything had changed!

—N. N. SUKHANOV

Ekaterina Breshko-
■ Breshkovskaya, a veteran
populist and the "little
grandmother" of the
Russian Revolution, with
her "grandson" and close
personal friend, Alexander
Kerensky.

First session of the newly
■ elected Petrograd Soviet,
now led by the Bolsheviks.

LEFT

Leon Trotsky, the new
■ chairman of the
Petrograd Soviet of Workers'
and Soldiers' Deputies.

The people give their vote
to radical leftists—
Bolsheviks, Anarchists, Left
Socialist Revolutionaries—
in local elections.

LEFT, TOP AND BOTTOM

Municipal elections in two
■ Moscow districts.

TOP RIGHT

Election day in Moscow at
■ the Soviet of Soldiers'
Deputies on Tverskaya (now
Gorky) Street.

CENTER RIGHT

Demonstrators demand:
■ "Proletarians of All
Countries, Unite! An 8-
Hour Working Day!"

BOTTOM RIGHT

Revolutionaries
■ demonstrating in
Turkmenia.

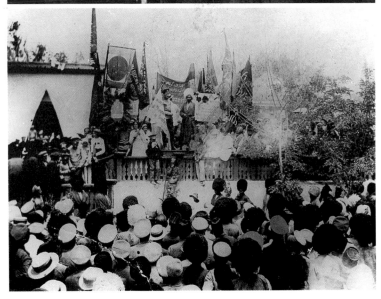

A food line in the center of Moscow at the corner of Tverskaya Street and Hunters' Row.

Pitchers in hand, women all over Russia line up for milk.

TOP

A detachment of Red Guards learning how to handle weapons.

BOTTOM

Red Guards of the Vulkan Factory, Petrograd.

LEFT

In Petrograd a line forms outside the Emil Tsindel Textile Company.

Radical workers, sailors, and soldiers quickened the pace of their revolutionary activities in early October. On 16 October Petrograd's most aggressive revolutionary elements formed a Military Revolutionary Committee. Acting out of the Smolny, where the Petrograd Soviet, the Bolsheviks, and other radical parties were headquartered, this group, led by Trotsky, set the revolution in motion. From 20–24 October it undercut support for the government, using subversive tactics rather than direct assault. The telegraph exchange, telephone switchboard, and electrical stations were taken and bridges and train stations were secured. Soldiers and sailors at key installations put themselves at the committee's disposal. Kerensky's troop support melted away; government headquarters, the Winter Palace itself, was guarded only by members of the women's battalion and a few military school cadets, and they fled when the cruiser *Aurora* fired a round of blanks at the palace. While his cabinet ministers cowered inside, Kerensky slipped away. There was some shelling, but no dramatic storming of the Winter Palace. Early in the morning of 26 October, Bolshevik Antonov-Ovseenko led some revolutionaries into its quiet halls; they arrested the last ministers of the Provisional Government and surveyed the damage done as the Revolution triumphed and the world's first socialist state was born.

A view of the Neva River from a bullet-shattered window in the Winter Palace after its capture by the Military Revolutionary Committee's troops on the night of 25–26 October.

RUSSIA 1917

OCTOBER

ОКТЯБРЬ

The government is tottering.
We must deal it the deathblow at
any cost. To delay action is the
same as death.

—V. I. LENIN

A symbolic exchange of banners between soldiers and workers, 1 October.

BELOW

Members of the Pavlovsky
■ Regiment hand their banner to workers of the Putilov Factory.

RIGHT

The banner of the Putilov
■ Factory: "Long Live the Russian Revolution as a Prologue to Social Revolution in Europe! Under This Banner We Pledge to Achieve a Brotherhood of All Nations. To the Heroes, the Pavlovsky Guardsmen, from the Workers of the Putilov Factory."

Братскій союзъ рабочихъ и солдатъ.
Обмѣнъ знаменъ Путиловцевъ и Павловцевъ 1-X 1917г.
Вручéніе адреса Павловцами Путиловцамъ.
31

"One has the feeling that the Provisional Govnment is in the capital of an enemy who has just completed mobilization. . . ." General Levitsky, an aide to Kerensky

ABOVE

A meeting of the Petrograd
■ Bolshevik military committee.

RIGHT

A Petrograd street on one
■ of the first days of the Revolution.

TOP INSET

Barricades block the road
■ leading to the Admiralty, 24–25 October.

BOTTOM INSET

A Red Guard patrol warms
■ itself on a Petrograd street. Photo Ya. Steinberg.

The Revolution begins.

ABOVE

Red Guards of the Putilov
■ Factory surrounding the
tank they seized from the
Junkers (young cadets), 23
October. They named it
Lieutenant Schmidt after a
hero of the 1905 revolution.
Photo P. Otsup.

LEFT

Red Guards on their way
■ from the Smolny to carry
out the orders of the
Military Revolutionary
Committee, 25 October.
Photo P. Otsup.

BELOW

The telephone exchange is
■ captured and occupied
by Military Revolutionary
Committee troops.

The Smolny, command
■ center of the Revolution,
was originally a finishing
school for girls of noble
birth.

LEFT

Red Guards of the Putilov
■ Factory on the steps of
the Smolny.

BELOW

At the Smolny gate,
■ security is tight.
Photo Ya. Steinberg.

The Winter Palace, where ■ the Provisional Government made its last stand, as seen from across the Neva River. Photo Ya. Steinberg.

Barricades of firewood in ■ the middle of Palace Square.

Junkers are among the last ■ protectors of Kerensky's tottering government.

Members of the Women's ■ Shock Battalion of Death also help guard the palace.

Sergeant T. Kirpichnikov (left), of the Volynsky Regiment, one of the first to go over to the side of the Revolution.

RIGHT

The Peter and Paul Fortress. The Winter Palace was shelled from here on the night of 25–26 October.

RIGHT INSET

The cruiser *Aurora*, which fired a single deafening round of blanks at the Winter Palace.

Shell-shattered windows of the Winter Palace.

On the morning of 26 October, photographer Ya. Steinberg took pictures of some of the nearly 1,000 rooms in the palace to document the destruction caused by the shelling and by the troops who had been guarding Kerensky and his ministers.

The Soviets come to power
in Petrograd.

TOP

Red Guards and
■ revolutionary soldiers
checking documents at the
Smolny.

BOTTOM

The fledgling Soviet
■ Government's fear of
counterrevolutionary actions
makes checking documents a
way of life.

LEFT

A demonstration honoring
■ the Second All-Russian
Congress of Soviets, at
which the Bolsheviks gained
a majority. Standing beneath
the banner in tie and glasses
is Bolshevik leader Anatoly
Lunacharsky, soon to
become Commissar of
Education.

All power may have gone to the Bolshevik-dominated Soviet in Petrograd, but as the revolution spread around the country, its supporters encountered much more opposition than in the capital. In Moscow, antirevolutionary elements formed a Committee of Public Safety and made a determined stand against the local Military Revolutionary Committee. Barricades were raised on major streets and squares, artillery guns bombarded the city. The two sides fought a bitter contest for possession of the Kremlin. Artillery shells pitted its massive walls, towers, and gates. The ancient fortress changed hands several times, but on 2 November Soviet forces captured it once and for all. Those who died defending the Revolution were buried as heroes at the base of the Kremlin wall. Even while the fight for Moscow was still raging, in Petrograd Lenin was forming the world's first socialist government. For a brief time it was made up exclusively of Bolsheviks, but under strong pressure from non-Bolshevik socialists it was soon reconstituted as a coalition of Bolsheviks and Left Socialist Revolutionaries. On 12 November elections of delegates to the long-desired Constituent Assembly began—the first free elections in Russian history and the last for more than seventy years.

Soviet power is hard won in Moscow. The traces of a fierce street fight are seen in this bullet-ridden phonograph-store window.

RUSSIA 1917

NOVEMBER

НОЯБРЬ

Slowly from the Red Square ebbed
the proletarian tide. . . . I suddenly
realized that the devout Russian
people no longer needed priests to
pray them into heaven. On earth
they were building a kingdom more
bright than any heaven had to offer,
and for which it was a glory to die.

—JOHN REED

Firemen demonstrating during the first days of the Revolution in Moscow.

BELOW

The battle was much more heated in Moscow than in Petrograd.

The battle lines are drawn.

BELOW

Artillery is set up on
■ Tverskaya (now Gorky)
Street to protect the
Moscow Soviet building.
Photo G. Goldstein.

TOP RIGHT

Barricades are raised on
■ Arbat Square in the heart
of old Moscow.

CENTER RIGHT

A column of Junkers
■ marching past the
barricades on Arbat Square.

BOTTOM RIGHT

Barricades block
■ Varvarskaya Square, not
far from Red Square.

The Kremlin changes hands
several times in a bitter
fight.

TOP

Members of the Moscow
Military Revolutionary
Committee retake the
Kremlin for the last time
on 2 November.
Photo A. Dorn.

CENTER

Red Guards on patrol
inside one of the
Kremlin's massive gates.

BOTTOM

The Nikolsky Gate was
badly damaged by
artillery fire during the fight.
Photo A. Dorn.

The Spasskaya Tower took several direct hits.

INSET

"**W**hite" Junkers guarding the Kremlin before revolutionary forces retook it.

The fight for Moscow leaves deep scars.

RIGHT

The staff headquarters of a Red Guard detachment was riddled with bullets.

TOP INSET

A building where a regional soviet met suffered heavy damage.

BOTTOM INSET

The Metropole Hotel, a favorite of foreign correspondents, was also badly hit.

BELOW

Red Guards patrolling the battle-torn streets.

A new tradition is established: burial of the Revolution's martyrs at the Kremlin wall.

ABOVE

Freshly dug graves at the ■ wall. The banner reads: "Glory to those who died a heroic death. . . ."

LEFT

Mourners make their way ■ past the Kremlin's ancient churches carrying their revolutionary banners.

LEFT INSET

Coffins draped in banners ■ are solemnly carried to the Kremlin wall.

Examining election posters for the Constituent Assembly, the first free elections in Russian history. The posters say: "Vote for the People's Freedom Party"; "Vote Ticket No. 7"; "The People's Socialist Labor Party" (with portraits).

RIGHT

Vladimir Ilich Lenin, leader of the new Soviet state. Photo M. Nappelbaum.

RIGHT INSET

Campaigning for votes in the Constituent Assembly elections.

The conquest of power by the Soviets throughout Russia came in the wake of Bolshevik victories in the capitals. Each city, town, and village made its revolution in its own way. In the final days of the final month of 1917, Russia was quite literally a land of revolution. On Lenin's initiative, the Congress of Soviets began acting on the reforms that radicals had been demanding since February. Capital punishment and private ownership of land was abolished. Class distinctions were invalidated. The banks were nationalized. Peace terms were declared and Trotsky was entrusted with leading a Soviet delegation to Brest-Litovsk for peace negotiations with the Germans. Neither he nor any of the other leading Bolsheviks, for that matter, had any diplomatic or governmental experience. They had to invent everything, a new form of government, even a new name: Council of People's Commissars. And the problems they faced were enormous: a country wracked by war; a breakdown in civil order; sabotage by enemies of the Revolution; virulent anti-Bolshevik propaganda; imminent civil war. There was, however, widespread enthusiasm for a new kind of life, a new kind of state, a bold leap into the future toward socialism and beyond to communism.

A worker, a soldier, and a ■ peasant hold a banner that reads: "Workers, Soldiers of All Nations, Demand an Immediate Peace. Long Live Soviet Power. . . ."

DECEMBER

ДЕКАБРЬ

TOP

Demonstrators in
■ Petrograd demand
"Recognition of Soviet Power
and the Soviet Government
by the Constituent Assembly."

BOTTOM

A rally for peace negotiations
■ with Germany. The
banner reads: "Long Live the
Social Revolution. Long Live
Socialism."

LEFT

A demonstration against
■ counterrevolutionaries
and for the Soviet
Government's peace plan.
"Death to the Enemies of the
People, the Kornilovites and
Kaledinites!!! Long Live
Soviet Power, which has
Paved the Way for Peace
among Nations."

Peace negotiations with Germany begin.

LEFT

Russian soldiers and their ■ wives cross no-man's-land to fraternize with German soldiers.

LEFT INSET

"**D**own with Offensives! ■ Long Live a Universal Peace!" demonstrators demand at a peace rally in Petrograd.

TOP RIGHT

Russian negotiators behind ■ German lines near Dvinsk.

BOTTOM RIGHT

The Soviet delegation ■ arrives in Brest-Litovsk; German representatives greet Lev Kamenev.

Combatting
counterrevolution
and sabotage.

TOP

Red Guards of the New
■ Lesner Factory
preparing to fight
General Kaledin's
counterrevolutionary forces.

BOTTOM

Firemen pumping wine out
■ of a cellar into the gutter
to prevent looting—and
drunkenness.

RIGHT

Felix Dzerzhinsky, head
■ of the feared political
police—the Cheka—
established six weeks after
the October Revolution.

A nationalized bank in
■ Moscow. Its old sign is
covered by a new one:
"Second Branch of the
People's Bank of the Russian
Republic."

The Council of People's
■ Commissars at the end of
1917. Lenin (center) is
chairman. Other important
members include Alexandra
Kollontai, commissar of social
policy (seated at Lenin's left),
and Joseph Stalin, commissar
of nationalities (standing at
Lenin's side).

Soviet soldiers in Moscow
■ at the end of the year,
marching forth under a
simple banner: "Communism."

AFTERWORD

Most of the photographs reproduced in this book come from the U.S.S.R. State Archival Fund—the national property and heritage of the Soviet people.

The life and activities of every nation are reflected in its documents. Man has always taken care to preserve the records of his history: they provide an inexhaustible source of spiritual strength and a vital link with past generations.

In the Soviet Union, as in most countries, the keeping of archives has a long history. Ancient chronicles bear witness to the fact that archives began to take shape as early as the Kievan Rus period in the tenth century. The majority of those documents, of course, did not survive to the present day. Over time, however, special repositories were established for the gathering and preserving of archival materials.

Broad legislation concerning archives was enacted in 1550, with the establishment of provisions for the handling and preservation of "state affairs." In the seventeenth century a series of decrees on the categorization and storing of such "state affairs" in departmental archives was put into effect. In Peter the Great's "Regulations on Colleges" of 1720, the tsar devoted an entire chapter to the "arrangement" of archives. By the beginning of the twentieth century a rather well-developed system of archival institutions was in place.

A new stage in the development of archives began after the October Revolution of 1917. The leader of our country, Vladimir Lenin, took great personal interest in archival institutions. On 1 June 1918, he signed a decree of the Soviet of People's Commissars, "On the Reorganization and Centralization of Archives in the RSFSR." As a result of this important state act, all archival documents in the country became the property of the government and the people. On this foundation the U.S.S.R. State Archival Fund was formed.

Today there are 3,273 state archives in the Soviet Union. They hold 340 million items, including priceless documents of ancient Russia, the Ukraine, Byelorussia, the Trans-Caucasus, the Baltic states, and Central Asia; chronicles, manuscripts, and other materials from the tenth through thirteenth centuries; documents that recount the history of the formation of the Russian state and the unification of Russians with other peoples; memorabilia of Peter the Great's sweeping reforms; material on the peasants' movements, the revolutionary struggle of the working class, and, of course, all stages of Soviet history: the Great October Socialist Revolution, the civil war, the military feats of the people during World War II, and the postwar reconstruction.

The state archives guarantee the safekeeping and proper inventory of documents; they oversee the selection of new documents and the organization of their use in the interests of society.

Soviet archival institutions maintain contacts with archival institutions all over the world. Every year some 250 scholars from abroad work in the state archives. The Soviet Union, as well as the Ukrainian and Byelorussian republics, are active members of the International Council of Archives.

Contacts and ties between Soviet and American archival institutions have existed for a long time. On the initiative of Soviet and American archivists, a collection of documents and materials, titled *Russia and the U.S.A.: The Establishment of Relations, 1764–1815*, was published. The next joint project in this series, *Russia and the U.S.A.: The Establishment of Relations, 1816–1865*, is currently being prepared.

In 1986, in connection with the General Agreement between the U.S.S.R. and the U.S.A. on Contacts, Exchanges, and Cooperation in Science, Technology, Education, Culture, and Other Areas for 1986–1991, and the Program for Cooperation and Exchanges between the U.S.S.R. and the U.S.A., Soviet and American archivists signed the Agreement and Protocol on Further Development of Joint Ventures in Archiving.

We proceed from the assumption that international cooperation helps in the exchange of archival experience, as well as in the building of trust, friendship, and mutual understanding, so needed in our restless times.

Fyodor Vaganov
Professor of History

BIOGRAPHICAL NOTES ON THE PHOTOGRAPHERS

KARL KARLOVICH BULLA (1853–1929)

Born in Germany, Karl Karlovich Bulla moved to St. Petersburg as a young boy. He was introduced to photography when he worked as a messenger for a company that produced photographic equipment. Twenty years later he opened his own photography studio in the fashionable Passazh shopping arcade and gained a reputation as the best photographer in the city. He specialized in portraits of the aristocracy and of eminent scholars, musicians, artists, and writers, including Fyodor Chaliapin, Ilya Repin, Leo Tolstoy, and Maxim Gorky. He is also renowned for a large series of photographs devoted to the everyday life of St. Petersburg at the turn of the century. As the events of the February Revolution unfolded, Karl Bulla was on the scene with his camera. From the window of his studio on Nevsky Prospect, he captured the ceaseless tide of demonstrators marching down Petrograd's main thoroughfare. In mid-July 1917 he and his wife moved to Estonia.

VIKTOR KARLOVICH BULLA (1883–1944)

The son of Karl Bulla, Viktor Bulla mastered the art of photography at a young age. His first assignment as a professional journalist was to cover the Russo-Japanese War of 1904–05 for the journal *Niva* (The Cornfield). Upon his return to St. Petersburg, he became interested in cinematography and founded the association Apollon, which produced newsreels and travel films. He never abandoned his original profession, however, and during the February Revolution he did not part with his camera. He captured some of the most dramatic moments of 1917, including the shooting of demonstrators by Provisional Government troops on 4 July. Right after the October Revolution, he became the head of photography for the Petrograd Soviet. He and his brother, Alexander, who was also a photographer, gave more than 130,000 negatives—all taken by the Bulla family—to the State Archives of the October Revolution.

YAKOV VLADIMIROVICH STEINBERG (1880–1942)

Yakov Steinberg began his career as a photojournalist at the turn of the century. By 1913 he was working for St. Petersburg's best illustrated journal, *Solntse Rossii* (The Sun of Russia). During World War I he was at the front photographing battles. But he is best known for his pictures of revolutionary events in Petrograd: workers', soldiers', and sailors' demonstrations; the feverish activities at the Smolny in October; the ransacked rooms in the Winter Palace after the Provisional Government was overthrown. In the 1920s Steinberg became head of Petrograd's Society of Artistic and Technical Photography. At a photography exhibition in the Academy of Arts in Leningrad, 1924, 300 of his photographs of the Revolution were shown—an impressive number and a telling indication of the importance of his work. More than 6,000 of his negatives are held in the Leningrad State Archive of Cinematography and Photography.

PYOTR ADOLFOVICH OTSUP (1883–1963)

Pytor Otsup was born into a middle-class St. Petersburg family. At age ten he was apprenticed to a portrait photographer and then became an assistant to V. Yasvoin, a prominent photographer in the capital. From 1900–17 he worked as a photojournalist for such magazines as *Niva, Rodina, Ogonyok,* and *Solntse Rossii*. During 1917 Otsup devoted all of his experience and talent to the revolutionary cause; his photographs of the Smolny in the days when the Military Revolutionary Committee was preparing to overthrow the Provisional Government are particularly memorable. After the Revolution he became head of the photo studio of the Russian republic's Revolutionary Military Soviet and later director of the photo studio of the All-Russian Central Executive Committee. He also continued his work as a photojournalist, recording many events of the civil war, including the raids of the First Cavalry and the suppression of the Kronstadt Rebellion. Pyotr Otsup's photographs of Lenin were printed in millions of copies and acquainted the world with the image of the first Soviet leader. They also influenced the way Lenin was portrayed by Soviet painters, sculptors, graphic artists, and actors. In a conversation with Otsup about photographing historic events, Lenin said, according to the photographer: "The lens captures history very well. History in photographs is clearer, more comprehensible. Not a single artist is capable of recording on canvas what the camera sees."

ALEXANDER FYODOROVICH DORN (1886–1956)

Working as both a photographer and a cinematographer, Alexander Dorn was one of the photochroniclers of the Revolution in Moscow. Among other events, his lens captured the dramatic and bitter fight for possession of the Kremlin and the burial of the dead in the Kremlin wall. During the civil war Dorn took part in the trips of the Central Executive Committee's propaganda trains to Central Asia and ships down the Volga and Kama rivers. He later worked for the All-Russian Photography and Cinematography Department. Unfortunately, many of his photographs of the Revolution did not survive World War II.

GRIGORY PETROVICH GOLDSTEIN (1870–1941)

Trained as a pharmacist, Grigory Goldstein began working as an illustrator for the Moscow newspaper *Utro* (Morning) in 1907. He then took up photography and became a photojournalist for another Moscow paper, *Rannee utro* (Early Morning) in 1915. During 1917 he chronicled the events of the October Revolution in Moscow with his camera: the barricades on the city's main squares, the fierce fighting, the shelling of buildings, the digging of fresh graves along the Kremlin wall. After the civil war he taught at the State Institute of Cinematography and worked as a caricaturist for the newspaper *Vechernyaya Moskva* (Evening Moscow), where he was head of the illustration department.

SELECT BIBLIOGRAPHY

WORKS IN ENGLISH ABOUT 1917

Abraham, Richard. *Alexander Kerensky: The First Love of the Revolution.* New York: Columbia University Press, 1987.

Avrich, Paul. *The Russian Anarchists.* Princeton, New Jersey: Princeton University Press, 1973.

———. *The Anarchists in the Russian Revolution.* Ithaca, New York: Cornell University Press, 1973.

Browder, Robert Paul, and Kerensky, Alexander, editors. *The Russian Provisional Government, 1917: Documents.* 3 vols. Stanford, California: Stanford University Press, 1961.

Burdzhalov, E. N. *Russia's Second Revolution: The February 1917 Uprising in Petrograd.* Bloomington, Indiana: Indiana University Press, 1987.

Chamberlin, William Henry. *The Russian Revolution, 1917–1921.* Vol. 1: *1917–1918: From the Overthrow of the Tsar to the Assumption of Power by the Bolsheviks.* New York: Macmillan, 1935. Reprint. Princeton, New Jersey: Princeton University Press, 1987.

Chernov, Victor. *The Great Russian Revolution.* New Haven, Connecticut: Yale University Press, 1936.

Daniels, Robert V. *Red October: The Bolshevik Revolution of 1917.* New York: Charles Scribner's Sons, 1967.

Deutscher, Isaac. *The Prophet Armed: Trotsky, 1879–1921.* New York: Vintage, 1954.

Ferro, Marc. *The Bolshevik Revolution: A Social History of the Russian Revolution.* London: Routledge and Kegan Paul, 1980.

Galili y Garcia, Ziva. *The Menshevik Leaders of the Petrograd Soviet in 1917: Between Social Realities and Political Strategies.* Princeton, New Jersey: Princeton University Press, 1989.

Getzler, Israel. *Kronstadt, 1917–1921: The Fate of a Soviet Democracy.* Cambridge, England: Cambridge University Press, 1983.

Gill, Graeme. *Peasants and Government in the Russian Revolution.* New York: Barnes & Noble, 1979.

Hasegawa, Tsuyoshi. *The February Revolution: Petrograd, 1917.* Seattle, Washington: University of Washington Press, 1981.

Katkov, George. *Russia 1917: The February Revolution.* London: Collins, 1967.

———. *The Kornilov Affair.* New York: Longman, 1980.

Keep, John L. H. *The Russian Revolution: A Study of Mass Mobilization.* New York: W. W. Norton, 1976.

Kerensky, Alexander. *Russia and History's Turning Point.* New York: Duell, Sloan and Pearce, 1965.

Koenker, Diane. *Moscow Workers and the 1917 Revolution.* Princeton, New Jersey: Princeton University Press, 1981.

Mandel, David. *The Petrograd Workers and the Fall of the Old Regime: From the February Revolution to the July Days.* New York: St. Martin's Press, 1984.

———. *The Petrograd Workers and the Soviet Seizure of Power: From the July Days, 1917 to July 1918.* New York: St. Martin's Press, 1984.

Mawdsley, Evan. *The Russian Revolution and the Baltic Fleet: War and Politics, February 1917–April 1918.* New York: Barnes and Noble, 1978.

Melgunov, S. P. *Bolshevik Seizure of Power.* Santa Barbara, California: ABC-CLIO, 1972.

Miliukov, Paul N. *The Russian Revolution.* Vol. 1: *The Revolution Divided, Spring 1917.* Gulf Breeze, Florida: Academic International Press, 1978.

Mstislavskii, Sergei. *Five Days Which Transformed Russia.* Bloomington, Indiana: Indiana University Press, 1988.

Rabinowitch, Alexander. *Prelude to Revolution: The Petrograd Bolsheviks and the July 1917 Uprising.* Bloomington, Indiana: Indiana University Press, 1968.

———. *The Bolsheviks Come to Power: The Revolution of 1917 in Petrograd.* New York: W. W. Norton, 1976.

Radkey, Oliver H. *The Agrarian Foes of Bolshevism.* New York: Columbia University Press, 1958.

Raleigh, Donald. *Revolution on the Volga: 1917 in Saratov.* Ithaca, New York: Cornell University Press, 1986.

Reed, John. *Ten Days That Shook the World.* New York: Vintage, 1960.

Rosenberg, William. *Liberals in the Russian Revolution: The Constitutional Democratic Party, 1917–1921.* Princeton, New Jersey: Princeton University Press, 1974.

Salisbury, Harrison, E. *Black Night, White Snow: Russia's Revolutions, 1905–1917.* New York: Doubleday, 1978.

Saul, Norman. *Sailors in Revolt: The Russian Baltic Fleet in 1917.* Lawrence, Kansas: Regents Press of Kansas, 1978.

Smith, S. A. *Red Petrograd: Revolution in the Factories, 1917–1918.* New York: Cambridge University Press, 1983.

Sukhanov, N. N. *The Russian Revolution, Nineteen Seventeen.* Princeton, New Jersey: Princeton University Press, 1984.

Suny, Ronald Grigor. *The Baku Commune, 1917–1918: Class and Nationality in the Russian Revolution.* Princeton, New Jersey: Princeton University Press, 1972.

Trotsky, Leon. *The History of the Russian Revolution.* 3 vols. New York: Simon and Schuster, 1932–34.

Tucker, Robert C., editor. *The Lenin Anthology.* New York: W.W. Norton, 1975.

Voline. *The Unknown Revolution: 1917–1922.* Montreal, Canada: Black Rose Books, 1975.

Von Mohrenschildt, Dmitri, editor. *The Russian Revolution: Contemporary Accounts.* New York: Oxford University Press, 1971.

Wade, Rex. *Red Guards and Workers' Militia in the Russian Revolution.* Stanford, California: Stanford University Press, 1984.

———. *The Russian Search for Peace.* Stanford, California: Stanford University Press, 1969.

Wildman, Allan K. *The End of the Russian Imperial Army.* Vol 1: *The Old Army and the Soldiers' Revolt (March–April 1917).* Princeton, New Jersey: Princeton University Press, 1980. Vol. 2: *The Road to Soviet Power and Peace.* Princeton, New Jersey: Princeton University Press, 1987.

INDEX

PHOTOGRAPHY CREDITS

JANUARY

1 New Year's Day.

9 Anniversary of Bloody Sunday, the massacre at the Winter Palace that started the 1905 Revolution. Lenin delivers anniversary address in Switzerland.

31 Scattered strikes in Petrograd factories.

FEBRUARY

14 Fourth Duma resumes after Christmas recess.

18 Strikes at the Putilov Factory in Petrograd.

19 Bread shortage begins in Petrograd.

23 International Women's Day. The insurrection begins as women demonstrate in Petrograd.

24 Strikes and insurrection spread.

25 Soldiers begin to support strikers. Left-wing newspapers are shut down.

26 Tsar dissolves Duma.

27 Provisional Executive Committee of the Petrograd Soviet of Workers' Deputies is formed. Duma members form a "Temporary Committee." Guards units mutiny.

28 Formation of Moscow Soviet of Workers' Deputies.

MARCH

1 Order No. 1 issued to army. Petrograd Soviet votes not to join in formation of Provisional Government.

2 Formation of Provisional Government. Tsar Nicholas II abdicates.

3 Grand Duke Mikhail renounces throne. End of Romanov Dynasty. Provisional Government publishes its program.

5 Petrograd Soviet authorizes cessation of strikes.

6 Strikes end. Amnesty for all political prisoners.

8 Tsar arrested.

10 Department of Police abolished.

11 General Alekseev replaces Grand Duke Nikolai Nikolaevich as commander of armed forces.

12 Abolition of death penalty.

20 Abolition of religious and nationality discrimination. United States enters the world war.

24 Introduction of bread rationing in Petrograd.

APRIL

1 Petrograd Soviet resolves to support Provisional Government.

3 Lenin returns to Russia on sealed train; issues April Theses.

8 Government authorizes use of troops to put down agrarian disorders.

18 May Day parades and demonstrations. Miliukov note on Dardanelles made public. The April Crisis begins.

20 Workers demonstrate against Miliukov and Provisional Government.

24 Bolshevik Party conference opens.

26 Deportation to Siberia abolished.

27 Law on freedom of the press.

29 Grain rationing declared.

MAY

1 Executive Committee of Petrograd Soviet approves participation of socialists in the government.

3 Miliukov resigns.

4 First All-Russian Congress of Soviets of Peasants' Deputies. Trotsky returns from exile in the Bronx.

5 First coalition government with socialist participation formed.

10 Eight-hour workday proclaimed.

22 Brusilov succeeds Alekseev as commander in chief.

25 Socialist Revolutionary Party Congress opens.

30 Prince Pyotr Kropotkin, anarchist leader, returns home.

JUNE

1 Admission of women to Russian bar.

3 First Congress of Soviets opens.

5 Provisional Government raids Durnovo villa, anarchist headquarters.

10 Russians retreat on southwestern front.

14 Government sets 17 August as date for elections to Constituent Assembly and 30 August as date for its convocation.

16 Kerensky orders an offensive in Galicia.

18 Russian offensive begins.

24 Introduction of student self-government in institutions of higher education.

25 Elections to Moscow municipal duma.

28 Russian offensive begins to falter.